In Praise of

Discerning the Voice of God
by the Leading of the Holy Spirit

"Tony provides a refreshing and enlightening approach to knowing the voice of God. Follow his guidance as he instructs you on how to let go and receive clear direction during peace or turmoil. All Christians, from the new believer to the more mature, will benefit from the wisdom shared in *Discerning The Voice of God by the Leading of the Holy Spirit*."

Darryl Bell
Founder of Hope and Exchange
International Best-Selling Author of *We Are Creators*

"Religion is a very sensitive topic, and in a very sincere and intelligent tone, Tony Douglas discusses his relationship with the higher power, whatever that may be. He calls it God. I call it a connection to something greater. Secondly, the idea that fear will never control you again, once you have that connection, is an important principle of getting what you want in life. Really, once you begin to live out of love and not out of fear, life is totally different. This book is not just for Christians, it is for the thinkers and for the doers who want to make their mark on this world and help others improve the quality of their lives. This book is for anyone who resonates with the power of intuition. A must-read and HIGHLY recommended."

Katia Stern
International Best-Selling Author of *You Were Born WOW*
Women's Empowerment Coach & Jack Canfield Protégé

"Great read and perfect to keep as a reference book. Tony Douglas is a man of God and this book is life-changing!."

Ann Collins
Best-Selling Author of *Hope, Loss, Encourage*

"I've been blessed to know Tony since 2013 and have always looked up to him for his God-centered demeanor. Tony is an accomplished former boxer and I can see the 'fight' is still in him—the desire to fight the good fight against the world, the enemy and his schemes by listening for the voice of our Creator in all things great and small. I feel fully blessed that Tony has listened to God's voice to write this book and to be our 'coach' and guide us on this most important journey. Tony leaves no stone unturned as he goes into great detail regarding the different ways Christians have either neglected to hear, have misunderstood or have correctly embraced discerning God's voice. A short but profound and powerful message Tony drives home in the first five chapters is how often even 'good' Christians sometimes rely on "reasoning" instead of doing the harder work of fully relying on the Lord. I am so looking forward to hearing God's voice more clearly through this valuable tool written by a great godly man. Tony, thanks for listening to our Savior and sharing with us the blessings that He Himself taught you! Here's to living a more powerful and effective life by *Discerning the Voice of God by the Leading of the Holy Spirit!*"

David Pertgen
Retired Police Officer
Anti-Money Laundering Compliance Associate

"Tony Douglas is a graduate of my Committed Author Program and he has committed to bring you a powerful message that is near and dear to his heart. This beautifully written book contains an important message for Christians who have a desire to know and hear the voice of God."

Peggy McColl
New York Times Best-Selling Author

"Tony Douglas has done a remarkable job teaching his readers the importance of hearing the voice of God. It is a deep spiritual dive that makes you ask yourself, 'What can I do to be better?' 'How can I make sure this is God's voice?' In reading this wonderful book, you will definitely find the answers. *Discerning the Voice of God by the Leading of the Holy Spirit* is a gift to all that will read it. Tony gives us a spiritual road map that will help us navigate the spiritual terrain and not only fine-tune our spiritual ear, but help us mature in the deep things of God."

Reverend Melodie Boone
Author of *Fearless*
Assistant Pastor of St. Mark A.M.E. Church, VA Beach, VA
CEO and Founder of Liberty Coaching and Consulting, LLC

"Minister Tony Douglas provides clear instructions, along with practical examples, on how to recognize and respond to the voice of God. Errors in this area can be detrimental to our Christian walk, creating unnecessary problems and failures. God wants to help us, and the voice of the Holy Spirit is a crucial means for Him to do so. Believers must make it a priority to know and properly respond to the voice of our Heavenly Father.

I strongly recommend that anyone needing to mature in recognizing and responding to the voice of God, take the time to read this book. Not only will it help you recognize the voice of God, but it will also shut down the voice of the enemy who wants to interfere with what God has to say to you. You will be blessed by reading this book, just as I was!"

Minister Reggie Isaac

DISCERNING
THE VOICE OF

GOD
BY THE LEADING OF THE
Holy Spirit

TONY DOUGLAS

Permission should be addressed in writing to Tony Douglas at
Tonydouglas611@gmail.com

Editor: Kathryn Young
kathryn@hasmarkpublishing.com

CoverDesign: Otis Lockhart
lifelegacies@gmx.com

Book Design: Anne Karklins
anne@hasmarkpublishing.com

ISBN 13: 978-1-989756-49-2

ISBN 10: 1989756492

I dedicate this book to my wife, Wanda, for your love, patience, and support. After 33 years of marriage, you're still the best partner for me.
I am looking forward to the second half of our life together.

TABLE OF CONTENTS

ACKNOWLEDGMENTS

First, I give thanks to **God**. Without him, this book would not be published. He kept me on track when things became extremely difficult. He carried me through some challenging days and provided his grace so that I could keep a made-up mind to finish what I started. I am thankful that He gave me his peace in the midst of life's storms. His peace enabled me to keep every obstacle under my foot. To God be the glory.

To **Wanda Douglas**, my wife and friend. All of these many years of being together, you have never wavered in your commitment to me. You have given up a lot to make my life much easier. I am truly privileged to be your husband, and I don't take that lightly. Your support and wisdom have enabled me to reach new levels in Christ. Thank you for your friendship and for fighting with me through every obstacle I faced. You are an exceptional mother and a general in the army of the Lord. I truly respect and honor your place in Christ.

To my children **Jordan and Adria**, whom I love dearly. Both of you have allowed me to be your father with uncompromising love for me. It means a lot to me that each of you still loves to hang out with your Daddy. Thanks for the many hours each of you spent listening to me teach you the principles in this book.

To my cheerleader and friend **Janice Thomas**. The countless hours of just listening and allowing me to run things by you really helped me to stay true to the spirit of the book. I am truly thankful for having you as a friend.

To my colleague **Tamisha Pumphrey**, who volunteered many hours of her time to set up the management of my social media campaign. Thank you so much for being there for me and for giving your expertise in this area. Your support and kindness will never go unanswered by God. May God multiply your generosity back to you in the form of your desire.

I would like to give a special thanks to my coach and editor, **Melodie Boone**. The completion of this book would not be possible without her. I remember praying, *God, I have taken this book as far as I could; send me the right person to help me complete it.* Melodie, you were the right person for me. I thank you for your professionalism, patience, and commitment to the details of this book. The many encouraging words you spoke enabled me to push through the tough times. You continued to give me the perfect balance of encouragement and challenging projects. You never wavered in your belief in me, no matter how much work needed to be done to complete this book. I will forever be grateful for your commitment to me.

I am very grateful to have **Otis Lockhart** as my book cover designer. His gift and creativity are unique. I chose him because I knew that he was sensitive enough to the Holy Spirit to create the design that I desired. He nailed it on the first design. Otis, thank you for your patience and the excellence you displayed throughout the process.

The scriptures quoted in this book are from the King James Version of the Bible.

FOREWORD

I have known Tony Douglas for over 30 years as his pastor and have watched him grow as a Christian, man of God, husband, father and a pillar of the church.

The book gives clarity to one of the most important subjects that pertain to a Christian—discerning the voice of God. Every believer has grappled or wrestled with this at some point in their life, and desires understanding and clarity in it. Reading this well-written, informative book will make things clearer, bring more confidence, and undergird your foundation on how the Spirit of God works with us.

Jesus clearly taught that it would be to our (Christians') advantage if He went away so the Holy Spirit could come to replace and represent Him as well as act on His behalf. It is critically and vitally important that the Holy Spirit's ministry be studied and that we learn to recognize Him in our lives. Tony Douglas has done some of the work for you.

May I encourage you to read and meditate on its contents and put it into practice. I know that this writing will inspire and motivate you to develop a relationship with the Holy Spirit and allow discernment of His voice to be prevalent in your life. It's an honor to recommend this book to you.

Pastor Robyn Gool
Victory Christian Center

PREFACE

Hello stranger! Thanks for opening up this book so that I could introduce myself. My name is Tony Douglas. It's not a mistake that you picked up this book. I believe that you have been led by the Holy Spirit at this point in your spiritual journey to find out for sure how you can know the voice of God for yourself.

There are several reasons why you were led to this book. The reasons don't matter as much as the fact that you are here, ready to learn and mature in your walk with God. Surely you have heard the old saying, "When the student is ready, the teacher will appear." Let's get one thing clear: I am not the teacher. The Holy Spirit is the teacher, and he is using this book as a resource to help you get the answers you need about knowing God's voice for yourself.

You may be experiencing some frustrations around this topic because of past failures and disappointments. Hopefully, when you read this book, God's peace will wrap you like a blanket. Finally, you have clarity and can understand how to recognize God's voice in a way that was never revealed to you before. The Spirit of God will open up your eyes so that you can see and open your ears so that you can hear. I believe that as you read this book, the spirit of wisdom and understanding will come to you. You will be able to see and hear clearly what you need to know.

My purpose for writing this book is to help Christians know the voice of God for themselves and not depend on anybody to give them a word from God. I have seen many individuals get misled, abused, and then backslide because they sought a word from God through other people. Depending on other people to tell you what God's will is for your life can be dangerous. Some have never recovered, and others took years to get back on their feet.

Most Christians do not know the voice of God for themselves, nor do they know how the Holy Spirit leads them to discern the voice of God. If they would allow the Holy Spirit to teach them, he will make it very simple and easy to distinguish the difference between God's voice and all of the other voices speaking to them daily. The Holy Spirit's job is to teach you all things. Discerning the voice of God is one of those things that you should ask the Father by the Holy Spirit to teach you. The Holy Spirit is willing and ready right now to assist you, but are you ready and willing to learn? The teacher will show up when the student is truly ready. The Holy Spirit is looking for students who are willing and ready to put the work in, no matter how long it takes.

In 2014, I personally took 18 months and studied nothing but the voice of God. During this time, I only heard messages that my pastor preached on Wednesdays and Sundays. My personal study time was spent learning the voice of God by the leading of the Holy Spirit. I am not saying that you have to do what I did, but for me, it was well worth the time I put in. Spending this amount of time was not my initial goal. I was only going to do 90 days, but the Holy Spirit unveiled so much of the word of God to me on this topic that I just couldn't get enough. I was extremely hungry, motivated, and excited about what I was learning. Revelation just kept coming at me repeatedly day after day. The practical application of what I was learning in daily living was made so easy for me by him that I wondered how I could have missed it all these years. The Holy Spirit made it so simple for me to understand when God was talking that my learning experience became life-changing. My life changed drastically, and my spiritual confidence soared. I possessed a tool that I could use anywhere at any time to be victorious in life. No matter what direction I was taking, I knew that I was hearing from God by the leading of the Holy Spirit.

So, as a result, this book was designed to help you know when God is talking to you, and when He is not. You will be able to discern God's voice by the leading of the Holy Spirit in every area of your life. Hopefully, I will be able to convey how simple it is to hear and know God's voice in a way that's easy to practice in everyday life.

Those of you who know his voice, I believe you will get a lot out of this book as well. You will get clarity and sharpen your discerning skills. It will become easier to hear and know his voice in a busy world that's pulling on you all day long. Being able to discern God's timing or season for your life will become simpler. Possessing the ability to know God's voice and follow him when faced with negative, unexpected, and volatile events is another benefit that you will gain.

I knew the voice of God prior to writing this book, but I was still unsure in some situations I faced. The high-risk volatile situations at times would give me problems. These are the types of situations where the risk of losing is so high that it causes you to be on an emotional roller coaster. The thought of being wrong costs too much. Every day people are faced with making life-threatening decisions. For example, what if you were faced with making a decision pertaining to a medical procedure of a loved one? This procedure has a 95 percent probability of leaving them paralyzed for the rest of their life. But you also know if they do not have the procedure, they will die. You are the only one who can make this decision, and their life is in your hands. If you are wrong, it will take years to recover from it. Because the risk is so high, your emotions are extremely unstable. What are you going to do? How are you going to handle this?

When I was faced with extreme situations, I needed to learn how to relax and be patient while hearing from God in the storm. It's easy to hear God when you are not in a storm. What if you are in a storm, and God wants you to stay and learn how to hear him to find your way out? What if finding your way out takes three to six months or more? How would you handle that?

God wants to teach us to be at peace in the storm. He wants us to trust him even though we are afraid and feel pressured to go in another direction. A time will come when you, as a Christian, will have to stand alone with God and receive no physical support from any individual. Until you can accomplish this by tuning out the noise of the storm and controlling your emotions, you will not become a Christian who effects positive change. You cannot allow yourself to be controlled by your senses.

This is the dispensation of the Holy Spirit, and it's his time on the earth to guide and teach the Church. That includes discerning the voice of God by his leading. It's not hard, but it takes practice and patience. It also takes courage to act on what you hear. It may appear foolish in the eyes of the world, and it might even look as though God is trying to embarrass you. But what you have to remember is that He is not trying to embarrass you or make you look foolish. Any time that you obey God, it always turns out to be advantageous for you. The end is always better than what we see in the present.

So, with that being said, let's get started learning how to discern the voice of God by the leading of the Holy Spirit.

INTRODUCTION

I became a Christian in May 1984. As a new born-again Christian, my heart's desire was to please God. I had a strong desire to know what the will of God was for my life. To please him and know what his will was for my life, it was imperative that I knew his voice. I desperately wanted to know the voice of God and was willing to do whatever it took to accomplish this. I had many questions, but no answers. For example, I wanted to know, what does God's voice sound like when He speaks? How can I recognize it? Is it a deep voice from heaven? How can I tell if it's God talking to me? Is this God, me, or the devil talking?

In this book, I'm going to share with you several principles the Holy Spirit taught me in the 18 months of studying how to discern God's voice. I did not study or meditate on any other Bible topic during this time. Personally, I wasn't interested in anything else because I believed that if I mastered this subject, my life would change in ways that I couldn't imagine. I strongly believe it's one of the most important things in the Christian life that can ever be discussed or taught. It's something that seemingly has eluded, frustrated, and confused most Christians. The simple but powerful principles that I'm going to share with you will enrich your relationship with God and draw you closer to him. It will bring increase into your life on many levels: spiritually, financially, physically, and emotionally.

I will teach you how to discern the voice of God by the leading of the Holy Spirit. If you follow these principles, your life will never be the same. You will become more of a blessing to the Kingdom of God and a huge problem for the kingdom of darkness. The world will be amazed at what God is doing through you. Most are looking for demonstrations of God's power through signs and wonders. Because of their carnality, these signs and wonders will be received as proof of how much God loves them. As Christians, we know the greatest expression of God's love was sending Jesus to die for the sins of the world. There is no greater love that can compare to what Jesus accomplished through his death, resurrection, and ascension. There is no greater sign or wonder that demonstrates his power and love for mankind. Once all people believe this in their hearts and say it out of their mouths, there wouldn't be anything that could stop them from surrendering their lives to God. Then you will truly see what the Bible says in Matthew 9:37b, "The harvest truly is plenteous, but the laborers are few."

When you know his voice, you will begin to increase your time of fellowship with him. Your relationship with God will become so rich that his peace will flow through you to the point that when you walk in the presence of others, it grabs their attention. They will smile at you and want what you have even though they can't quite understand what it is. People will gravitate to you and reveal secrets about themselves, which they've never shared before with anyone. There will be times that you will know things about people without them telling you. When you talk to them, they will wonder how you know these things. They will ask, "How did you know that when I didn't tell you?" It is because you know God's voice. He is able to reveal things to you at the same time that you are talking with them. It's a beautiful communication network that happens between God, you, and the individual. This is a seamless process that can happen all of the time instead of every now and then. These are just a few of the many wonderful things that will happen to you as a result of knowing God's voice and being led by the Holy Spirit. If you don't know his voice, you will continue to struggle spiritually. You will remain frustrated because things are not working out like you thought they would.

CHAPTER 1

GOD, IS THAT YOU SPEAKING TO ME?

Over the years of observing Christians, I've noticed that they would fall into different categories or groups as it pertains to knowing God's voice. In the first five chapters of this book, we will look at five groups.

The first group includes those Christians who don't know God's voice. This group includes individuals recently saved as well as those who have been Christians for many years. Specifically, I am talking about the new born-again Christians who just gave their lives to the Lord. These individuals are very curious and zealous about the ways of God. All of us were a part of this group when we first got saved. I remember asking questions: What does God's voice sound like? How do I know it's God talking to me? I would get answers from the older Christians saying, "It's a still small voice."

An answer like that was very confusing to me as a baby Christian. Let's think about this for a moment. First of all, I don't know his voice, and secondly, I don't know what to listen for or what I'm supposed to hear. I eagerly wanted to know God's method of communicating with me outside of the preaching of his word. But now, I am being told that "it's a still small voice" that I am listening for. The older Christians have just made it more difficult for me than they could have imagined. So, how am I supposed to hear a still small voice when I don't even know what I am listening for or where to listen? Is God's voice up there in the clouds or within me? Where is God's voice coming from, and where should I look? For many years these questions were never answered effectively. Jesus clearly states in the book of John, "My sheep know my voice and a stranger's voice they will not follow." I'm aware of what the Bible says in John 10:3-5, but let's look a little closer into this scripture and find out what Jesus is saying.

> "To him the porter openeth and the sheep hear his voice: and he calleth his own sheep by name and leadeth them out. And when he putteth forth his own sheep he goeth before them and the sheep follow him for they know his voice. And a stranger will they not follow, but will flee from him for they know not the voice of strangers."

This couldn't be the absolute truth if you took it at face value. There has to be something that is missing that we just don't understand or see. Personally, I have followed a stranger's voice many times as I have matured in the things of God, and so have you. Yet the scripture says, "A stranger's voice they will not follow." If that's the case, whose voice were we following when we thought we were hearing from God? That blunder we made that really embarrassed us could not have been God. Surely, God is not out to make us look bad. The truth is that we followed a stranger's voice. We did not follow the voice of God. You might be wondering how could that be when the scriptures plainly state that it would not happen? Let me explain. All of our lives, we are programmed to make reasonable decisions, to do things that make sense. The conscious mind is where we reason things out. To put it more plainly, we are conditioned to follow the voice of reason. We are trained to hear from the *outside in* which is based on our five physical senses: touch,

2

taste, hearing, smell, and sight. We are never trained to hear from the *inside out*.

Our spirit knows God's voice, but our conscious mind does not. Have you ever experienced a time in your life when you said, "I knew I should not have done that; something told me not to do it." We all have experienced this at different times in our lives. From a child to an adult, our conscious minds have never been trained to hear God's voice. This is why the Bible says in Romans 12:2:

> "And be not conformed to this world; but be ye transformed by the renewing of your mind, that ye may prove what is that good and acceptable, and perfect will of God."

We can't obey God if we don't recognize that He is speaking to us. We have allowed our conscious mind to govern our lives from a very early age. That's why it is easy to follow the voice of a stranger. As Christians, we consistently follow the voice of our conscience because it makes sense to us. This is good old common sense and reasoning having preeminence in our lives. Everything must make sense to us, and if it doesn't, it's dismissed quickly. Your conscious mind is the gatekeeper or warrior that fights day and night to maintain control over you against anything that doesn't make sense. It is relentless in its attack against faith or anything outside of the realm of the physical senses. Anything that threatens its control over you must be dealt with. Our conscious mind has never been trained to hear God from the inside out. Ephesians 4:22-24 states:

> "That ye put off concerning the former conversation the old man, which is corrupt according to the deceitful lusts; and be renewed in the spirit of your mind; and that ye put on the new man which after God is created in righteousness and true holiness."

Our conscious mind must be renewed by the word of God so that we can discern and obey his voice when He speaks. The Bible says in Revelation 2:7a, "He that hath an ear let him hear what the Spirit saith unto the churches." God knows that you have ears to hear. That should give you an indication that God is not talking about our physical ears. He's talking about our spiritual ears or inner ears that are designed to hear into the spiritual realm. Your inner ears were made to discern good and evil with ease. Your inner ears were made to hear God and to follow his voice.

For example, as babies, God gives us five physical senses: touch, taste, smell, hearing, and sight. These physical senses were designed by God and given to us to navigate our lives in the physical world. Our conscious mind is in charge of these senses. But God has also given us a spirit that is designed to navigate the spiritual world. The spirit of man was designed to be in fellowship with God, to hear and obey him. Also, the spirit was designed to have complete control over a man's mind, will, emotions, and body. The spirit of man was designed strictly for God and to have preeminence in the physical world. In other words, the spirit of man was to be the dominant force of human life.

Hopefully, at this point, you understand more clearly what the Bible says in John 10:3-5. Remember, it's the spirit that will not follow a stranger's voice, but your conscious mind will because it's been trained to follow voices that operate within the five physical senses. Your spirit will always follow God because it was designed to follow him. We must train our conscious mind to submit to our spirit and resist our mind when it wants to go in a different direction. The more we bring our conscious mind into subjection to our spirit, the less of a fight we will have. The conscious mind will obey you because you are consistent with being obedient. Repetition is the key to causing it to submit. Your conscious mind understands this activity because that's how it learns. It's an effective way of bringing it under control. The Bible says in Romans 12:2:

> "And be not conformed to this world: but be ye transformed by the renewing of your mind, that ye may prove what is that good and acceptable, and perfect, will of God."

To renew the mind and be transformed takes a lot of repetition in confessing and meditating on the word of God. This means the information and process must be correct to produce change. You must have correct knowledge that is consistently being meditated on daily so that old thoughts can be replaced with new thoughts. This will cause the mind to be changed and the transformation of your behavior to take on a new path in life.

CHAPTER 2

THE HIT AND MISS GROUP

The second group of Christians is the hit and miss group. They're not sure what the voice of God sounds like. When asked the question, "Do you know the voice of God?" most of them would say, "I think I do, but I'm not a hundred percent sure. Sometimes, I feel like I do, and other times, I just don't know for sure who is talking to me." These are the Christians who get it right sometimes, but most of the time, they miss it badly. This is the hit and miss group.

This group of Christians is consistently confused and frustrated. They've had some great experiences with God on a novice level. Of course, as a novice, you must be careful not to allow the devil to get you to become haughty. Walking in pride is not easily detected as a novice. The devil creeps in with pride, and the individual begins to think they are more than what they are. The Bible clearly tells us in Romans 12:3:

> "For I say, through the grace given unto me, to every man that is among you, not to think of himself more highly than he ought to think; but to think soberly, according as God hath dealt to every man the measure of faith."

As Christians, we cannot afford to live in pride. The devil will use our successes as an opportunity to get us to think more highly of ourselves than we should. This is a dangerous place to be in because sooner or later, shame and destruction will happen if the person doesn't change. There are a couple of scriptures that confirm this. So, when the devil tries to get you to walk in pride, remember these two verses:

> "When pride cometh, then cometh shame: but with the lowly is wisdom." (Proverbs 11:2)

> "Pride goeth before destruction, and a haughty spirit before a fall." (Proverbs 16:18)

The hit and miss group has experienced some embarrassing moments. For example, I've personally seen these Christians tell people that God told them to do a particular thing, and it turned out not to be God at all. They became heartbroken and shamed to the point where it was difficult for them to show their faces in public again. They became confused and frustrated. They didn't understand what they did when they got it right or how they missed it when they got it wrong. Their desire to please God is so strong that when they miss it, it's extremely difficult for them to forgive themselves. So, they hold on to each failure until it starts to eat at their relationship with God.

These failures pile up, and because they don't let them go, the devil takes advantage of this opportunity by reminding them of every failure they've made. He begins to accuse them day and night. He makes everything look really bad between them and God. He uses their zeal to please God against them. He makes it appear as though God is angry at them and will never use them again. This group of Christians is trying very hard to please God and to make him proud of them. They don't realize that it's OK to make a mistake while learning his voice. They also are in bondage to the false teaching that God is a punitive God who's watching to punish them when they make a mistake.

Even though these Christians experienced some success, the misses caused major setbacks in their lives that took the wind out of them. In some cases, it took years to recover from the losses that occurred. With so many repeated misses, eventually, fear sets in, and they just stop trying. They begin to make decisions based on their flesh and how they feel about a particular thing. Or they rely on good old common sense. They eventually become very carnal-minded without being aware of it.

Some older Christians, who have been saved for many years, fall into this same group. I've witnessed many of them backsliding because they became weary and confused about what they thought they heard from God. The setbacks were too much for them to bear. So, they became followers of their flesh, and it led them into the world again. The Bible says in Romans 8:5-8:

> "For they that are after the flesh, do mind the things of the flesh; but they that are after the Spirit, the things of the Spirit. For to be carnally minded is death; but to be spiritually minded is life and peace. Because the carnal mind is enmity against God: for it is not subject to the law of God, neither indeed can be. So then they that are in the flesh cannot please God."

The consistent failure of not pleasing God takes its toll on them. They ask themselves, "What's the use of trying to live for God? It's too hard. I am messing up all of the time. How can I say that I am a Christian, and I'm constantly falling into sin? I just can't do this anymore; it's too hard."

9

So, they leave God and go back to living the life they're familiar with, a life ruled by their senses. It is a life that will end up in spiritual death.

CHAPTER 3

THE UNSEASONED IN
HIGH-RISK VOLATILE SITUATIONS

The third group includes Christians who know God's voice, but they are unseasoned in high-risk volatile situations. I just thought about something that needs to be mentioned here before moving on. Many Christians think that God is putting them in bad situations to teach them something. No! God does not put you in bad situations to teach you anything. But He will allow it to happen for many reasons. He will get you out of it if you trust him.

Life itself has a way of testing you. Negative, unexpected events happen to all of us. Also, you have the devil who is the enemy of your soul; he will cause negative things to happen to you. There is only so much he is allowed to do, and you must remember that you have authority over him. Resist him, and he will flee (James 4:7). As long as you are on the right side of the dirt, still alive and breathing, you are going to have trials and tribulations. But be of good cheer because you have overcome the world with its trials and troubles. This is why you see bad things happening to good people, whether they are Christians or non-Christians. Yes, the devil causes some of it but not all of it. People blame God and the devil for a lot of things they have nothing to do with. Sometimes it's just life and other times it's just making bad decisions.

Sometimes this third group of Christians is faced with situations where the loss is greater than their tolerance level. They find it difficult to stand on what the word of God said. As a result, they revert back to listening and *obeying the voice of reasoning*. It's all about good decision-making skills. What God has said has been dismissed and never to be brought up for consideration at all. Following God will cost too much. The loss that could take place, as a result of following him, is too great.

Let's look a little closer into the backdrop of how the minds of this group of Christians are challenged. They are quick to acknowledge that they know the voice of God. But when they are faced with personal challenges that create extreme pressure, they are immediately exposed. The magnitude of the problem causes them to question their ability to hear God clearly. They experience many questions and statements that plague their minds day in and day out: Is God telling me to do this? What if I am wrong? Is this God or me? I just don't know. I have too much to lose if I miss it. I can't afford to be wrong and miss God.

They become afraid of the new challenge. Confusion and doubt begin to set in, and what they thought they knew becomes lost in the battle of the mind. They begin to mistrust their ability to hear God or the things that were taught to them by the Spirit of God. The constant attack of questions in their minds causes faith to become weakened. These questions cause doubt to come into their minds like the waves of the sea being blown by the wind and tossed to and fro. The Bible says, "A double-minded man is unstable in all his ways." (James 1:8). At this point, fear sets in, and paralysis takes place.

What usually happens at this point is that the individual looks for external help wherever they can find it. It's not that these individuals don't know the voice of God; it's a simple fact that they are not seasoned yet with high-risk situations that are extremely volatile. They have not faced the major league challenges of life where they are still able to hear God's voice in the storm. The major league challenges are the types of situations that cost a lot if you miss God. It can cost money, time, reputation and relationships. In some cases, it takes years to recover. For example, a teenager doesn't know how to handle the same challenges an adult faces. That's because teenagers are not seasoned enough in life to navigate through the different situations that challenge them mentally, emotionally and physically. Because of a lack of experience, they come out on the other side, traumatized. This is what happens to many Christians who are not seasoned in high-risk situations that are extremely volatile. Let's take a look at an example in the Bible, where Peter faced a high-risk situation that was extremely volatile. In Matthew 14:23-31, the scripture says:

> "And when he had sent the multitudes away, he
> went up into a mountain apart to pray and when the
> evening was come, he was there alone. But the ship
> was now in the midst of the sea, tossed with waves: for
> the wind was contrary. And in the fourth watch of the
> night Jesus went unto them, walking on the sea. And
> when the disciples saw him walking on the sea, they
> were troubled, saying, it is a spirit; and they cried out for
> fear. But straightway Jesus spake unto them, saying, Be
> of good cheer; it is I; be not afraid. And Peter answered
> him and said, Lord, if it be thou, bid me come unto thee
> on the water. And he said, Come. And when Peter was
> come down out of the ship, he walked on the water, to
> go to Jesus. But when he saw the wind boisterous, he
> was afraid; and beginning to sink he cried, saying Lord,
> save me. And immediately Jesus stretched forth his
> hand, and caught him, and said unto him, O thou of
> little faith wherefore didst thou doubt?"

Let's examine this passage of scripture closely to observe how Peter handled the high-risk volatile situation in which he found himself. The wind was blowing so hard that it caused the waves to toss the ship. Once Peter stepped out of the ship and walked towards Jesus, he began to fear for his life. He saw, heard, and felt the boisterous wind; and fear and doubt flooded his soul. He allowed himself to be ruled by his five physical senses. Fear and doubt caused him to sink. Peter found himself in a position that he was unaccustomed to. He was out on the water alone with Jesus and too far from the ship to reach back and hold on for safety. He became temporarily distracted and feared for his life. Mentally and emotionally, Peter lost it. Matthew 14:30 says, "he cried, saying, Lord, save me." Jesus had to grab his hand and pull him up quickly, or he would have drowned. Peter was unseasoned in high-risk volatile situations that threatened his life.

Now, let's look at how David handled a high-risk volatile situation that threatened his life when he defeated Goliath. The Bible says in I Samuel 17:4-10:

> "And there went out a champion out of the camp of the Philistines, named Goliath, of Gath, whose height was six cubits and a span. And he had an helmet of brass upon his head, and he was armed with a coat of mail; and the weight of the coat was five thousand shekels of brass. And he had greaves of brass upon his legs, and a target of brass between his shoulders. And the staff of his spear was like a weaver's beam; and his spear's head weighed six hundred shekels of iron: and one bearing a shield went before him. And he stood and cried unto the armies of Israel, and said unto them, Why are ye come out to set your battle in array? am not I a Philistine, and ye servants to Saul? choose you a man for you, and let him come down to

me. If he be able to fight with me, and to kill me, then
will we be your servants: but if I prevail against him,
and kill him, then shall ye be our servants, and serve
us. And the Philistine said, I defy the armies of Israel
this day. Give me a man, that we may fight together."

Goliath presented himself morning and evening for forty
days waiting for a soldier from the army of Israel to challenge
him. But they were afraid of Goliath and did not respond to
his challenge. David heard about it and went forth to challenge
Goliath. King Saul told David that he didn't stand a chance
with Goliath. David was a young boy, and Goliath had been a
man of war since his youth. King Saul was very concerned that
David would die fighting Goliath. But David had something
that King Saul didn't know about. David had faith in God, and
he was seasoned in high-risk volatile situations. This is what
David said in I Samuel 17: 34-36:

> "And David said unto Saul, Thy servant kept his
> father's sheep, and there came a lion, and a bear,
> and took a lamb out of the flock: And I went out
> after him, and smote him, and delivered it out of
> his mouth: and when he arose against me, I caught
> him by his beard, and smote him, and slew him.
> Thy servant slew both the lion and the bear: and this
> uncircumcised Philistine shall be as one of them,
> seeing he hath defied the armies of the living God."

David handled his high-risk situation perfectly. Let's examine David's character closely. Sure, physically, he didn't stand
a chance of defeating Goliath, and his life was at risk. But what
he had was faith and experience with God. He wasn't afraid to
verbalize it to King Saul or Goliath. He never allowed the size
of Goliath nor what he said intimidate him. He stayed mentally and emotionally strong. The battle was over so quick that

Goliath never saw what hit him. David defeated Goliath and demonstrated how seasoned he was with handling high-risk volatile situations.

Seasoned Christians, with experience in major life-threatening issues or situations that could cause their reputations to be ruined, don't buckle. When they are threatened with losing everything they have built, they continue to stand and not give up. Until you stand your ground against these types of challenges, you will not obey God's voice when He is trying to get you to step out into unfamiliar territory. He wants to take you on a journey that will change your life and affect the lives of others. But maturity has to take place for him to do so. You must be willing to stand alone with God and trust him no matter how great the challenge. The experience that you gain through facing numerous challenges with God will cause a trust in him that supersedes anything that you will ever face in your future. But first, there must be a detachment from reasoning things out. You must make a stand, and until you do, you will struggle to hear and obey God in high-risk volatile situations.

You must have courage when facing these types of volatile situations in life. If you don't, your transition to the next level will be very painful. The mental and emotional stress could cause you to remain stuck in the transitional stage versus successfully moving into the spiritual place where God has predestined you to be. Many Christians are in this spiritual stage with their relationship with God. They know God's voice and have become seasoned, but they are stuck in a transitional phase.

CHAPTER 4

THE TRANSITIONAL PHASE

The fourth group includes Christians who know God's voice and have become seasoned, but they are in a transitional phase. They are moving from being unseasoned in high-risk volatile situations to the transitional phase, and they are stuck in the middle. They have finally realized that to grow, they must stand with God alone in tough times and watch him bring them through. Jesus experienced a tough time when He was in the Garden of Gethsemane. He told his disciples in Matthew 26:38, "Then saith he unto them, my soul is exceeding sorrowful, even unto death: tarry ye here, and watch with me."

Jesus struggled mentally and emotionally. In the Garden of Gethsemane, Jesus had to stand alone before God. The battle was so intense that an angel was sent from heaven to strengthen him. Jesus was the perfect example of how to submit to God while experiencing mental and emotional distress. Jesus said, "Not my will, but thine be done." (Luke 22:42). He initially did not want to experience what was necessary to redeem man. His love for his father and the father's love for man was stronger than the anguish He was going through. Philippians 2:8 says, "And being found in fashion as a man, he humbled himself and became obedient unto death, even the death of the cross."

Jesus understands what we go through when facing tough trials. He demonstrated to us that giving up our life and submitting to the will of God is more profitable for us than to succumb to our flesh and emotions. Paul says in Acts 20:24:

> "But none of these things move me, neither count
> I my life dear unto myself, so that I might finish
> my course with joy, and the ministry, which I have
> received of the Lord Jesus, to testify the gospel of
> the grace of God."

Paul is saying it doesn't matter what I have to go through. I will complete the plan that God has for me. I will not value my life above his will. If I'm stoned or if I die, so be it. The will of God is more important than trying to save my life momentarily.

In our Christian walk with God, each of us has been in a place where we had to decide to move forward or hold on to what we know. Some of us have failed the test, and others have moved on. This is a very tough place to be in because you desire to move forward with God and obey his voice, but *the pull to hang on to what you know is sometimes greater than moving forward.*

The individuals who are in the transition phase have experienced many victories, and they feel good about themselves. But they also know that if the trial had lasted just a little longer, they would have buckled and reverted back to relying on the voice of reasoning and the advice of other people. They would have missed the opportunity of learning how to stand in the midst of the storm and relying on God to bring them out.

One of the challenges facing this group is how to endure to the end when facing extreme, prolonged high-risk situations. It's very difficult to handle these types of situations because of the amount of pressure that is put on the mind, emotions, will and body. It is exhaustive. We are expected to be able to deal with it for a week or a month. But when it lasts three months to a year or longer, it's a whole new level of fighting. We must be prepared to fight this long if we are going to experience moving to a new level in God. This new level is a place where only a few are living. They are experiencing the fullness of his blessings because they have learned to endure to the end.

In the past, this group has experienced being a victim of a few major setbacks, which caused them to internalize what they suffered. These internalized experiences constantly arise when they are faced with whether they should obey what God told them or rely on the voice of reasoning. The constant reminder of being a victim plagues them and makes it harder to stand their ground. Many times, they are stuck between two decisions: to obey God or to rely on what they think is best. This is why *the transition from unseasoned in high-risk volatile situations to the transitional phase is so tough.*

Most Christians never make it past this stage. They won't let go of the crutch of reasoning when they go through prolonged tough times because it's difficult for them to let go of something they know and have been trained to do all their lives. This type of change is tough psychologically. These individuals live and die, never reaching group 5, who I call The Masters.

CHAPTER 5

THE MASTERS

The fifth group includes Christians who have mastered hearing God's voice. They know his voice very well and have experienced numerous victories. They are not afraid of facing the unknown or how huge the challenges are that face them daily. These individuals understand how to endure to the end and wait patiently on the Lord. This group of Christians understands what the scripture in II Timothy 4:7 says: "I have fought a good fight. I have finished my course. I have kept the faith."

But as we look a little closer at this group of Christians, they have a more menacing challenge that faces them than the other groups that we have previously discussed. This menacing challenge is *disobedience* to the voice of God. On this level, disobedience comes with a huge penalty. The challenge they have is obeying God's specific instructions. Sometimes, they follow part of what God says and some of what they want to do. At other times, they may even put off what God told them to do until later. It's easy to put off what God wants you to do now, so you can complete something else He told you to do. Sometimes God wants you to do what He said now and not later when it's convenient for you.

For example, the Bible tells the story of Moses' disobedience and the consequences in Numbers 20:1-12:

> "And why have ye brought up the congregation of the Lord into this wilderness, that we and our cattle should die there? And wherefore have ye made us to come up out of Egypt to bring us in unto this evil place: It is no place of seed, or of figs, or of vines, or of pomegranates; neither is there any water to drink. And Moses and Aaron went from the presence of the assembly unto the door of the tabernacle of the congregation, and they fell upon their faces: and the glory of the Lord appeared unto them. And the Lord spake unto Moses, saying, take the rod and gather thou the assembly together, thou and Aaron thy brother, and speak ye unto the rock before their eyes; and it shall give forth his water, and thou shalt bring forth to them water out of the rock, so thou shalt give the congregation and their beasts drink. And Moses took the rod from before the Lord as he commanded him. And Moses and Aaron gathered the congregation together before the rock, and he said unto them, hear now, ye rebels; must we fetch you water out of this rock? And Moses lifted up his hand and with his rod he smote the rock twice and the water came out abundantly, and the congregation drank, and their beasts also. And the Lord spake unto Moses and Aaron, because ye believed me not, to sanctify me in the eyes of the children of Israel, therefore ye shall not bring this congregation into the land which I have given them."

Moses struck the rock twice instead of speaking to the rock. Moses knew the voice of God, but he chose to do what he wanted to do. He was frustrated with the people, which caused him to do something other than what God told him to do. God wants us to obey even the smallest things He asks of us. He does not want us leaning to our own understanding. Neither does He want pressure from people to push us to the point of disobeying him. Moses' disobedience caused him to pay a huge price. God told him that he would not lead the congregation into the promised land. Moses was not permitted to enter the land that was flowing with milk and honey. What a sad ending to the life of a great leader.

Another example is Adam and Eve in Genesis 3:1-19. Adam and Eve knew the voice of God but chose to disobey his commandment "not to eat of the tree of knowledge of good and evil." They knew about the penalty of death for doing so. God told them, "If you eat of this tree you shall surely die." Knowing the consequences did not stop them from eating the forbidden fruit. Because of their willful disobedience, sin and death were passed down to all men. This was the ultimate penalty for their decision. But thank God for Jesus Christ who died for our sins. He delivered us from death, hell, and the grave. The shed blood of the Lamb put us back in right standing with God. Now we have victory over sin because Jesus has freed us from a sinful nature.

Let me make this point very clear: *just because you know the voice of God doesn't mean that you will obey him every single time.* From time to time, this group misses it too. But their misses are very seldom. These individuals are *extremely disciplined* and have exercised full control over their flesh and emotions. But because they are human and are not perfect, they do struggle every now and then with their emotions and flesh.

As we have seen in the lives of Moses and Adam and Eve, when you get to this level, the price of disobedience sometimes comes with major consequences. The cost is very high.

But thank God for his grace, which is extended to every group of Christians that we discussed. No matter where you are within each group, God's grace will be enough to help you to continue forward even when you blow it or want to quit.

As I have matured in God, I have seen how He handles a new convert versus a seasoned Christian. As I have explained about the different groups in Chapters 1-5, his grace and patience are there for each Christian. But the cost is different because of the knowledge that each of them has of God. I have also seen how new and seasoned Christians use natural symbols to get directions from God. We will talk in the next chapter about what they are and how they are used to ascertain God's direction.

CHAPTER 6

PHYSICAL SYMBOLS

There were several questions I had as a new babe in Christ that you may have had as well, such as: How would I know what to do, when I didn't have a clue? How would I know when God is directing me to do something? I was told by mature Christians in the Lord that I would get a *green light* on the inside of me, and that meant I should do it. I was also told that I would get a *red light* on the inside, and that meant don't do it. I also remember being told that I would get a *check in my spirit.*

These types of answers just made me more confused and frustrated. Finally, I realized by observing these Christians over several years that each one of them meant well, but they didn't know the voice of God either. They were just repeating something they heard somebody say or what they had read in a book. They had no clue as to how this knowledge could be applied to their lives. So, they became like little parrots, repeating things they heard but had no revelation.

As I watched their lives over many years, I saw one big blunder after another. They were saying God told them to do this or that. What I realized was that many of them pretended to know the voice of God, but in reality, it was just in words only. This realization was very discouraging to me. I longed for someone who could teach me what was meant by these symbols: green light, red light, and a check in my spirit.

Today, I am going to save you a lot of time and frustration in trying to figure it out by yourself. These symbols are very easy to interpret. They are extremely useful for determining God's direction for your life.

What do green light, red light, and a check in my spirit mean? First of all, it doesn't have anything to do with your feelings. God will never lead you by your feelings. I will explain this in great detail later in the book. Let's compare these symbols to our traffic light system just to keep things simple. The green traffic light signal is telling us to go. We have the right of way, and therefore, we do not have to worry about any cars causing an accident with us. There is a sense of assurance, safety, and peace. This comes from knowing that other people are obeying the stoplight. It's a law, and you are confident that the law will be obeyed by the people driving the other cars. You believe they will not run the red light. From a spiritual perspective, let's see how it compares to our traffic light system.

Green Light

The term green light means *peace*. It means to go forward because peace is ruling or governing you. The Bible says in Colossians 3:15a, "Let the peace of God rule in your hearts."

This symbol of a green light gives an individual a sense of safety to move forward in a certain direction. First, before a green light changes to a red light, there is a yellow light. The yellow light means caution, slow down, and prepare to stop. It's not for you to speed up and run the light. The red traffic light signal tells us to stay still and wait patiently on the green light.

Red Light

A red light means *stop and wait*. It signifies unrest or uneasiness about doing something or going in a certain direction.

We need to stop and be patient by waiting on God to give us peace (a green light) before going in a specific direction. The Bible says in Psalm 37:7a, "Rest in the Lord and wait patiently for him."

To wait on God and rest in him can become very challenging for us. We live in a time where we want things to happen quickly. If it takes any time to acquire what we want, we become impatient. We need to be patient and discipline ourselves to wait on God to come through for us. Psalm 27:14 tells us to "Wait on the Lord: be of good courage and he shall strengthen thine heart: wait I say on the Lord." God will give us the strength to be patient while we wait on him to bless us. That's good news! God gives us everything we need to be victorious. Many times, we are impatient with God because He does things in his own time. Over the years, I have discovered that his timing is not the same as mine.

Have you ever wondered why God doesn't bless us sooner rather than later? He is all-powerful and all-knowing. Plus, He doesn't answer to anyone. There isn't anyone who could hinder him, so why should it take so long? My answer to these questions is this: we need to accept the fact that God can do whatever He wants to do, whenever He wants to do it. There is nothing we can do about it. So, we might as well get with his program and abandon ours.

Check in My Spirit

The terms red light and green light are no longer used much in Christian circles. But the term "check in my spirit" is still being used. Have you heard someone say this? I am going to share with you in simple terms what it means. Hopefully, you will understand and be able to walk this out in your relationship with God. I do not want you ignorant or confused.

A check in my spirit means a *hard or abrupt stop* in a direction. You should *turn away from or avoid* going the route you

27

were beginning to take and go in a different direction. It's the Holy Spirit preventing you from going in one direction and redirecting you to follow a different route. The Bible gives us a great example of this in Acts 16:6-8:

> "Now when they had gone through Phrygia and the region of Galatia, they were forbidden by the Holy Spirit to preach the word in Asia. After they had come to Mysia, they tried to go into Bithynia, but the Spirit did not permit them. So passing by Mysia, they came down to Troas."

When the Holy Spirit redirects you, this is called a check in your spirit. Paul and his companions were on their way to the province of Bithynia, but they got a check in their spirits by the Holy Spirit. The Holy Spirit prevented them from going in a direction that seemed right to them. He redirected them to bypass Mysia and go to Troas.

I remember when my wife and I were buying our first home. The Holy Spirit gave me a check in my spirit concerning which house to purchase. When Wanda and I got married in 1988, we were staying in a small two-bedroom apartment. One thing we loved doing together was going to home shows. This is where a home builder would display different houses they built. They would allow the public to view them in hopes that someone would purchase a home. We thoroughly enjoyed these shows and continued to go on a regular basis. It gave us vision and helped us to determine what we wanted in our home when we were ready to purchase. Both of us knew the apartment that we were living in was temporary. Even though Wanda knew this, she really struggled staying there. She did not like the neighborhood, and the apartment was too small. She prayed about it and allowed God to help her with her attitude. God spoke to her and said, if she couldn't make this her home, she would not get to her dream home. She made the adjustment, and we moved to a house in 1989.

After one year of being there, the owner gave us the opportunity to buy the house. The owner was giving us a great deal and was willing to do whatever it took for us to purchase the house. My wife was extremely happy about this opportunity. In the past, as a single woman, she had moved thirteen times in fifteen years. She wanted to settle down in a home and not have to move again. What she really needed was security.

As Wanda started gathering the necessary documents needed by the lender, I got a check in my spirit. I perceived in my spirit these words: *this is not it*. God was saying this is not the house. I told Wanda, "This is not the house. We are not buying it. Call the lender and homeowner and let them know that we are not buying the house." She was very disappointed. She asked me if I was sure about God saying that this is not the house. I said yes, I was sure. She could not believe that we were not buying this house. She said OK, and it appeared as though we were in agreement – at least that's what I thought. Two weeks later, I received a call from the lender about a scheduled closing date. I told them that I was not aware of a scheduled closing date. After I asked the lender a couple of questions, I told them to cancel the loan. We are not going to buy the house. I found out that my wife had the lender continue to process the loan after we had talked about not buying the house. She was hoping that I would change my mind and go ahead with the closing. But I was not going to disobey God. I knew with a certainty that God told me this was not the house.

I confronted her about it, and she admitted what she did was wrong. I reemphasized that we were not buying the house. I told her that I was calling the homeowner to let her know as well. After I said this, my wife had a major emotional meltdown. She cried for three days. During this time, I prayed for her and left her in God's hands. After the three days were up, she came out of her room, and she apologized to me. She said, "I knew it was not the right house, but because of moving so many times, I wanted a permanent place to live." I told her I understood and that I loved her. I asked her, "Are you ready to go get the house that is meant for us?" And she smiled and said, "Yes."

The house that Wanda was trying to get was a three-bedroom 1300 square foot house. The house that God blessed us with fifteen months later was a five-bedroom 4200 square foot house. Praise God!

So, what is the lesson here? Follow the check in your spirit. Remember, a check in your spirit is a *hard or abrupt stop* in a direction. You should *turn away from or avoid going* the route you were beginning to take and go in a different direction. That check in my spirit was an abrupt stop. I was led to go in a different direction. You have to stand firm on what God tells you even if your spouse or someone close doesn't agree with you. Don't be moved by emotions. It would have been extremely easy for me to be controlled by my wife's emotions. If I allowed that to happen, she would not be enjoying the house that God had for her.

Allowing the Holy Spirit to redirect you by a check in your spirit is very important in your walk with God. We don't always know what's up the road waiting for us as we are going about our daily lives. But if we pay attention to the Holy Spirit, he will direct our steps and cause us to be successful in everything we do.

These physical symbols were mentioned often by Christians in the past, but they are not used as much today. I wanted to give you information about them just in case you heard these terms. I don't want you to be confused about what they mean and how they are used. So, when you hear or read references to green light, red light, or check in my spirit, it's all about discerning the voice of God by the leading of the Holy Spirit.

CHAPTER 7

BE QUIET, LISTEN, AND
DO WHAT YOU ARE TOLD

There are three basic things you must do before you can discern the voice of God properly by the leading of the Holy Spirit. The Bible says in James 1:19, "Wherefore my beloved brethren, let every man be swift to hear, slow to speak, slow to wrath." To discern the voice of God properly, we must be quiet, listen, and do what we're told to do.

Has either of your parents ever told you, "If you don't be quiet and do what I told you to do, you're going to be in big trouble"? What they are saying is, "Don't talk while I'm talking. Listen and go do what I told you to do the first time, and don't let me have to repeat myself."

Be Quiet

To listen to God properly, we must "be quiet" and stop talking so much. You will never hear what God is saying unless you learn to be quiet. How can you hear him if you are consistently talking when you think you are praying? All you're doing is wanting to be heard because you think what you have to say to God is more important than what He has to say to you.

We have taken the scripture I John 5:14-15 to another level, which has gotten us into a bad place spiritually. It's become very disrespectful to God. Let me explain. The Bible says in I John 5:14-15:

> "This is the confidence that we have in him, that if we ask anything according to his will he heareth us: And if we know that he hear us, whatsoever we ask we know that we have the petitions that we desired of him."

We are quick to make sure that we are quoting the scriptures correctly. It's important that we have all spiritual bases covered because we want our needs to be met. Most of the time, we quote at least two or three scriptures or more and then finish it up with thanksgiving and praise in Jesus' name. Once that's done, we walk away. Generally speaking, we do not take the time to listen to anything God has to say. We just want to make sure that we are heard. Frankly speaking, we are not interested in what He has to say. We may not say it out of our mouths, but our actions speak louder than our words. While we are doing all of the talking and not listening, God is saying, "Would you please be quiet and let me say something? Can I at least get a word in? I have the answer to your prayers if you just listen."

But instead of listening, we run off to do our own thing. We leave God to work on meeting our need as though He's our servant. In a little while, when we check back in with God, we want everything to be in order as we have requested it. When it hasn't happened in the time frame that we think it should have, we start pulling God on the carpet. We say things like, God, what happened? Why is my need not met? You said in your word that you supply all my needs. We start quoting the word all over again. We leave his presence mad at him because He didn't do what we asked him to do. So, we walk away from him again, not listening to anything He has to say. Unbelievable, right? But we do this all the time, far more than we realize.

Listen

The Bible says in Mark 4:23:

> "And he said unto them, take heed what ye hear: with what measure ye mete, it shall be measured to you and unto you that hear shall more be given. For he that hath to him shall be given and he that hast not from him shall be take even that which he hath."

This scripture is an indication that information will be coming at you consistently from different places. Many voices will be talking to you daily. You need to take heed to what you hear and how long you hear it. And from whom you hear it. You need to be able to discern the source of the information and the validity of it. If you are listening to information that is unreliable or false for a prolonged period, it will take away accurate knowledge and cause you to think and believe wrong. Then, your corresponding actions will follow.

If the information or voices come from a pure source, then it will be measured back to you with increase. You will think accurately, and your corresponding action will be in alignment. So, beware if you don't discern properly. The things which you have will be taken away from you because you will inevitably make the wrong decision based on false information, which will cause you to lose something you had. The devil is the father of lies, and the truth is not in him. He is an unreliable source. Your conscious mind (the voice of reasoning) as it pertains to spiritual things is an unreliable source. This is why we must filter information through our spirits by the word of God and not our head.

We must make sure that we take time out of our busy schedule to listen to God talk to us. But it has to be a certain type of listening. We must make *attentive listening* a priority with God. With our busy schedules and the fast-paced world we live in, this can be very challenging.

First of all, you have to understand what attentive listening is. Attentive listening is engaging your entire soul. It's surrendering your mind, emotion, will, and your physical body to be at one with the other person when you listen to them. You must engage every part of you to pay attention to the other person. To listen to God appropriately, *we must quiet our minds, stabilize our emotions, and submit our will to listen to him.* We must allow his words to saturate us so that we become connected to him. You can become so focused on what is being said, that time seemingly stands still. Time is not an issue with God, nor should it be with you. What should only matter is being in the moment with him. It's him talking to you and you listening to him, and him talking to you and you listening to him. Did you notice that I repeated myself? This is because I want to emphasize you listening and not talking.

In these moments, you will know when to talk to him, if at all. You will perceive it in your spirit. The time you spend being quiet and listening to him is extremely enlightening. As you develop your listening skill with God, He will give you plenty of time to talk. Remember, if you really want to grow spiritually in your relationship with God, you must talk less and listen more. We have a lot to learn from God, and there is so much He wants to teach us. Let's not waste time talking. It's to our advantage if we listen first and talk later.

Do What You're Told to Do

I remember when I was a little boy, and my mother would ask me, did you hear what I said? I would reply, "Yes, ma'am."

She would then say to me, "Why didn't you *do what I told you to do?*" I knew at that point I could be in trouble, depending upon the answer I gave. Sometimes, I didn't want to do what she said right then, because I wanted to do it when I got ready. But of course, I wouldn't say that to her. Not doing what I was told to do, when I was asked by her to do it, caused me to face the consequences. This is also similar to our relationship with God. When He gives us instructions, He expects them to be acted upon immediately. Our feelings do not have anything to do with his expectation of obedience from us. This is something that we must keep in mind at all times.

It is important to listen to what God has to say. But it is of the utmost importance to do what He says the first time He speaks to you about it. The Bible says in James 1:22-24:

> "But be ye doers of the word, and not hearers only, deceiving your own selves. For if any be a hearer of the word, and not a doer, he is like unto a man beholding his natural face in a glass: For he beholdeth himself and goeth his way and straightway forgetteth what manner of man he was."

A person who is a listener only is self-deceived. These individuals forget who they are and to whom they belong. The 28th chapter of Deuteronomy talks about how the doer of God's word is blessed. It also talks about the person who just hears and is not a doer of his word. This person is cursed. Let's make sure that we are doing the basic things to recognize God's voice. God wants us to be quiet, listen, and do what we're told to do.

CHAPTER 8

HEARING FROM THE INSIDE OUT

The Bible says in I Corinthians 2:14, "The natural man receives not the things of the Spirit of God for they are foolishness unto him: neither can he know them because they are spiritually discerned." Revelation 2:7a says, "He that hath an ear let him hear what the Spirit saith unto the churches."

There is a distinct difference between your natural ears and your spiritual inner ears. You can be in a conversation with a person, and you're listening attentively with your natural ears; and at the same time, you can hear God talking to you about that individual. God's voice is so clear because you are hearing with your spiritual inner ears. You cannot accomplish this with your natural ears.

For example, if two people are talking to you at the same time, you will not be able to fully understand what either of them is saying. Eventually, you will say, "Wait, one person at a time. I can't hear both of you at the same time." But when you are in a conversation with another person, and God is talking to you, you can hear the other person and God clearly at the same time. That's because you are listening with two different ears.

All of our lives, we were trained to hear from the outside in. We were never trained to hear from the inside out. For example, as I have stated previously in this book, from the time we were born, God gave us five physical senses: touch, taste, smell, hearing, and sight. These physical senses were designed by God and given to us to navigate our lives in the physical world.

The soul of a man must be trained to recognize and obey the voice of God. Basically, it's the conscious mind of the individual that must be taught to hear and submit to the voice of God by the inner witness of the Holy Spirit. The conscious mind is the part of each person where reasoning controls every aspect of that individual's life.

The problem that we face as Christians is not God's fault; it's ours. We must take the time to train ourselves to hear God's voice. There is nothing wrong with our spiritual inner ears. They are working perfectly. The fact of the matter is that we have put plugs in them. The plugs are the voices of the flesh, emotions, and reasoning. These voices cause so much chaos and distraction until it becomes extremely difficult in hearing anything from God.

We have been trained to obey these worldly voices at all cost because we've been taught that they will keep us safe. We have become very skilled at discerning and obeying them. It's a miracle that God can get anything through to us. This is why we must be quiet before God and practice hearing his voice. You will not become effective at this if you are distracted consistently by the cares of this life. I know that we have to take care of things, but we must find the time to spend with God to train us to hear him. If you don't, you will continue to be a carnal Christian ruled by his or her senses. What a miserable way to live a Christian life.

But God has also given us a spirit that is designed to navigate the spiritual world. The spirit was designed to be in fellowship with God. Also, it is a conduit to release the power of God on the earth. The spirit of man was designed strictly for God to manifest his presence and have the preeminence in the physical world. In other words, the spirit of man was to be the dominant force of human life.

Your spirit knows the voice of God. The goal is to train your conscious mind to hear God's voice from your spirit. Your conscious mind has been ruling you your entire life. Therefore, it will not give up its position as ruler so easily. Because the voice of God is foreign to your conscious mind, it will fight intensely to maintain its control over you. Knowing God's voice means that you can't live your life being ruled by your senses or *sense-ruled*. God requires you to walk by faith and not by sight. This belief doesn't make sense to the conscious mind. It's foreign and totally out of character for you to do something like that. Remember, all of your life, you have been led by your senses and not your spirit. Therefore, expect a fight because you're going to be in one whether you want to be or not.

The Bible admonishes us in Galatians 5:16 to walk in the Spirit so that we don't fulfill the lust of the flesh. And to be spiritually minded is life and peace. This sounds like a victory to me. We don't have to be sense-ruled if we don't want to be. Being sense-ruled will lead to premature death. I want to have life and peace. What about you?

The conscious mind must be trained to become accustomed to God's voice. This takes time and discipline. Don't fool yourself into thinking this is going to happen quickly. It will not! Your conscious mind will give you all kinds of problems. That's because it's carnal. The Bible says in Romans 8:5-8:

> "For they that are after the flesh do mind the things
> of the flesh; but they that are after the Spirit the
> things of the Spirit. For to be carnally minded is
> death; but to be spiritually minded is life and peace.

Because the carnal mind is enmity against God: for it is not subject to the law of God, neither indeed can be. So, then they that are in the flesh cannot please God."

When our conscious mind is ruling us, we do all sorts of ungodly things. Its primary function is to be the *controlling force* in our life. It fights against spiritual things because it doesn't understand them. For the conscious mind, spiritual things don't make sense. It has to maintain its position of absolute control to continue being the primary decision-maker of human existence. These are just a few reasons why we should do what the Bible says and be transformed by the renewing of our minds. We can do this by meditating on the word of God daily. While continuing to do this, the word of God becomes alive in our spirit. Our thinking begins to change, which affects our behaviors.

CHAPTER 9

HOW TO TRAIN YOURSELF TO HEAR FROM GOD

Training Myself to Hear from God

The Bible says in Psalm 46:10, "Be still, and know that I am God: I will be exalted among the heathen, I will be exalted in the earth." God said, be still and know. Know what? That I am God. God is not our earthly mother or father, nor our employer or rich relative. These roles are limited in their power, but God is unlimited. He is the Almighty God who can do anything but lie or fail. God is saying be still and know who I am. Once we know who God is, then we will begin to trust him more. Trusting God allows him to manifest his presence through us. Then He will be exalted in the earth among the heathen. They will see through you that He alone is God, and there is no other like him.

If you are not willing to be still, you will never know what you need to know from God, when you need to know it. You will not be able to hear him because you are predominately on the move all the time. You're too busy with the cares of this world and the lust of other things. These external voices dictate to you the what, when, where, who and why. They tell you *what* you're going to do, *when* you're going to do it, *where* it's going to take place, *who* is going to be involved, and *why* it's going to be done this way.

To hear from God, you must know what his voice sounds like and where it comes from. You may be surprised to know that his voice sounds like your voice. It's not a deep voice speaking to you from the clouds. God speaks to us from the inside, not from the outside. Yes, He can speak audibly whenever He chooses, but it's very rare. When God speaks, his voice comes from within us. When you hear your conscience talking to you, where does it come from? It comes from the inside of you. So does God's voice. I am going to repeat it again: *God's voice sounds like your voice. He speaks to us from the inside, not from the outside.* When the devil speaks to you, what voice do you hear? Is it a deep, scary voice? No, his voice sounds like your voice. All of the voices we hear throughout the day sound like our own voice. The voices of the flesh, our emotions, our reasoning, the devil, and God, all use our conscious mind as a conduit to speak to us.

Our job is to distinguish or understand the nature of the voices that we are hearing. We need to make sure that what we obey is in alignment with the word of God. If it isn't, discard it and move on. Here are a few guidelines to consider when confirming the voice of God.

First, ask yourself, *Does the voice I hear line up with the word of God?* There are many voices that enter our minds throughout the day. If the voice that we hear is directing us to do something outside the boundaries of God's word, we should not obey it. Therefore, we have the responsibility to know his word for ourselves. We must become students of the word of God. Knowing God's word helps us to trust God's word because He cannot lie. The Bible states in Titus 1:2, "In hope of eternal life, which God, that cannot lie, promised before the world began." Also, Hebrews 6:18a says, "That by two immutable things, in which it was impossible for God to lie."

Secondly, ask yourself, *Does it take faith and courage for me to step out and do what I believe God is telling me to do?* I John 5:4 states, "For whatsoever is born of God overcometh the world: and this is the victory that overcometh the world, even our faith." Habakkuk 2:4b states, "The just shall live by his faith." When we are faced with situations beyond our abilities, it takes faith in God to overcome them. Faith is the spiritual power that God wants us to use every day. Faith is how Christians should live their lives daily. Living by faith is a requirement from God. He knows that faith will overcome anything that you will face in life. We must trust him and realize that He knows what's best for us.

Thirdly, *Does it go against the voice of reasoning or human logic?* The Bible says in Isaiah 55:8-9, "For my thoughts are not your thoughts, neither are your ways my ways, saith the Lord. For as the heavens are higher than the earth, so are my ways higher than your ways and my thoughts than your thoughts." God's thoughts and his ways are on a higher level than ours. He doesn't think on a human level. That's why it's extremely difficult for us to understand him. When we read the Bible, it appears to be a mystery to us. God wants us to obey what is written in the Bible, but it doesn't make logical sense. We will never be able to understand the thoughts and ways of God with our intellect. God reveals himself to us by his Spirit. The Comforter, which is the Holy Spirit, will teach us all things (John 14:26). We understand the thoughts and ways of God by the Holy Spirit.

Lastly, ask yourself, *Do I have peace and an inner knowing in my spirit about it?* The Bible says in Colossians 3:15, "Let the peace of God rule in your hearts." God's peace will always be present when He is directing you. If his peace is not present, stop and wait. Only go in the direction where his peace rules. John 2:20 states, "For ye have an unction from the holy one and you know all things." You will have an inner knowing that this is the direction you should pursue. The inner knowing and the peace of God will be present to confirm your direction.

To hear from God, you must gain control of your conscious mind. It's about being able to control your thoughts and become laser-focused on God's word. Learning how to focus your thoughts and get control of your mind is paramount. Practicing the simple technique that follows will allow you to control your thoughts and be able to focus on whatever you want. Being in control of your conscious mind is the major issue here. Taking back control and doing it whenever you want is pivotal to your success as a Christian.

Learning How to Focus Your Thoughts

First, you need to turn off your phones, computers, and the TV for ten minutes. These items cause you to be distracted. Then, just sit and be quiet. Be in the moment of silence. You must quiet the mind by focusing on what you hear around you. Focus on the sounds around you and then pick one of them to listen to. This focus allows you to control your thoughts and keep your mind from running off in different directions. You will be amazed at the things you have missed on a daily basis. There is so much life happening around you that it's easily missed by your busyness. Practicing this simple technique allows you to gain and stay in control of your thoughts. Doing this enables you to focus your mind on what you want to hear instead of what your mind wants you to hear. It teaches you to be patient in the silence so that God can speak to you. When He says something, write it down. Don't trust it to your memory at first. Even if you are experienced at knowing the voice of God, it won't hurt to write it down.

If we are honest, all of us have missed following specific instructions from God. We wondered why things didn't work out as we expected. Later, we found out through prayer that we forgot to do something that seemed small in our eyes. Everything God tells us is important, no matter how insignificant it appears to be. The problem is that we simply forgot something He said! We trusted our memory, which can and will fail us at some time or another. This mistake can cost you more than you want to pay and can be a very expensive lesson. I still write down some conversations that I have with God, and some I don't.

I've noticed over the years that it is easy to make a mistake and misinterpret what I thought God said. I assumed He meant one thing when He meant something different. Also, writing enables me not to miss the small details of the conversation. I am very encouraged when I use these conversations as a journal. It allows me to look back and remember all of the things He's brought me through. This practice builds confidence and a heart of gratitude toward God.

If you are new at learning to hear the voice of God, it would be wise to write your conversations down. Through practice, this helps you to identify who you are listening to. You become familiar with how God talks to you. You can distinguish and categorize the voices that talk to you daily. This knowledge helps you identify whether it's God talking to you or the devil disguising himself behind your senses.

In the next chapter, you will learn how to recognize who is talking to you. You will also learn the nature of these voices and the methods used to direct you to success or failure. Familiarizing yourself with these voices will enable you to make quick adjustments in the direction you're taking. You won't have to wonder if it's God or the devil talking to you. So, let's take a look at these voices and dispel the confusion. I want you to see with clarity so that you don't become weak in your faith.

CHAPTER 10

VOICE OF THE FLESH

The Bible says in I Corinthians 14:10, "There are as it may seem many voices in the world and none of them is without signification." There are five basic voices from a spiritual perspective that speak to us as Christians. They are the voices of the flesh, emotion, reasoning, the devil, and God.

Let's talk about the voice of the flesh. Romans 8:5, 13 says, "For they that are after the flesh do mind the things of the flesh; but they that are after the Spirit the things of the Spirit. For if ye live after the flesh, ye shall die: but if ye through the Spirit do mortify the deeds of the body, ye shall live."

The flesh is all about the physical pleasures of life. These are the things that make me feel good physically, such as drugs, sex, and food, just to name a few. The flesh is stimulated by the five physical senses, and it becomes stronger as it's fed by the senses: what it hears, sees, touches, tastes, and smells. If you look too long, touch the forbidden, and hear things that are unfruitful, your flesh will speak to you. It will cause you to bend to its selfish desires if you do not resist it.

What a person sees, if not controlled, gives power to the flesh; and they begin to yield their members to the works of unrighteousness, as the Bible says in Romans 6:13 "Neither yield ye your members as instruments of unrighteousness unto sin: but yield yourselves unto God, as those that are alive from the dead, and your members as instruments of righteousness unto God."

Your flesh has a voice, and it will speak to you along the lines of physical pleasures. It doesn't have to be sexual, either. It could be something as simple as having a desire for a certain food. This food is causing health issues, but you crave the taste of it. Even though you know it's unhealthy, you eat it anyway.

For example, I used to eat a loaf of bread a week. I had to eat bread with every meal. This was just the way I was raised as a young boy. Every meal had bread on the plate. So, of course, I carried this unhealthy tradition into my adult years. Sometimes, I would eat five pieces of bread at dinner. The voice of my flesh would say, "You need to get another piece of bread to finish this last little bit of food on your plate." This is after I had already eaten four pieces. In the past, I would eat at least three pieces of bread with Chinese food. I didn't understand why people would look at me strangely when I would do this. Later, I understood that it was an uncommon practice to eat any bread with Chinese food. My body craved bread, and it caused me to be out of control. The habit of overeating bread was a work of the flesh. The voice of the flesh convinced me that I needed bread to be satisfied or to enjoy my meal. Thank God, I finally got control of this issue after many years. I am no longer in bondage to the voice of my flesh in this area. When my flesh tells me to eat more bread, I resist it and walk out my victory. I am free, and I let the devil and my flesh know who's in control. Being in control of my flesh is liberating.

"Now the works of the flesh are manifest, which are these; adultery, fornication, uncleanness, lascivious- ness, idolatry, witchcraft, hatred, variance, emulations, wrath, strife, seditions, heresies, envying's, murders, drunkenness, raveling's, and such like: of the which

DISCERNING THE VOICE OF GOD

I tell you before, as I have also told you in time past,
that they which do such things shall not inherit the
kingdom of God." (Galatians 5:19-21)

Did you notice that strife is mentioned as a work of the
flesh? That means the voice of the flesh can cause you to enter
into strife with another person. To be in strife is to exhibit
vigorous opposition, bitter conflict, or hostility toward someone. When two people are in strife, they are not listening to
understand the other person. They are listening only to coun-
teract or defend their own interest or point of view. The Bible
gives us a good example of this between Paul and Barnabas in
Acts 15:35-41:

> "Paul also and Barnabas continued in Antioch,
> teaching and preaching the word of the Lord, with
> many others also. And some days after Paul said unto
> Barnabas, let us go again and visit our brethren in
> every city where we have preached the word of the
> Lord and see how they do. And Barnabas determined
> to take with them John, whose surname was Mark.
> But Paul thought not good to take him with them,
> who departed from them from Pamphylia, and went
> not with them to the work. And the contention was
> so sharp between them, that they departed asunder
> one from the other: and so Barnabas took Mark, and
> sailed unto Cyprus; and Paul chose Silas, and departed,
> being recommended by the brethren unto the grace
> of God. And he went through Syria and Cilicia,
> confirming the churches."

Here we see two Christian brothers who are leaders in the
Christian community in strife over John Mark. Paul did not
want to take him with them because John Mark departed
from them and went back to Jerusalem (Acts 13:13). Paul was

disappointed in John Mark and did not trust him. The Bible doesn't state the reasons why John Mark left them or whether he even told them he was leaving. But one thing that we can see is how it affected both Paul and Barnabas. There was a huge amount of contention and opposition between them. As stated before, when two people are in strife, the only thing that matters to them is their point of view and what is in their best interest.

Selfishness and pride are at the root of strife. Strife caused these two men who worked so well together to separate and go in different directions. These men were used mightily by God as a team. They lost sight of this simply because they could not come to an agreement about John Mark.

Now, let's look at how the voice of the flesh played a part in causing this story to end in strife. We have established, according to Galatians 5:19-21, that strife is the work of the flesh. Note that the voice of the flesh and voice of emotion are partners in crime. When you see one, the other is consistently present. I can imagine when Barnabas said that he was taking John Mark with them, something rose up within Paul. It wasn't the Holy Spirit either. It was anger, which opened the door for the voice of the flesh to express itself. I can imagine Paul asking, what do you mean you want to take John Mark? He left us when we needed him the most. He can't be trusted. How do you know that he won't do it again? I can imagine Barnabas reminding Paul that everybody makes mistakes. John Mark deserves a second chance. Give him a chance to prove himself. Of course, both of them have a great defense as to why he should stay or come with them.

So, one word led to another, and both of them became emotional. The strife was so great between them that separation was the only solution at the time. The Bible clearly states in Philippians 2:3, "Let nothing be done through strife or vainglory; but in lowliness of mind let each esteem other better than Themselves."

Paul and Barnabas should have esteemed each other better than themselves. They should have listened to one another so that a peaceable resolution could be agreed upon. They didn't give each other a chance. They could have dropped the conversation. This approach would have allowed them time to get their flesh and emotions under control. Then God's wisdom could have been received as to what should be done with John Mark. They needed a moment to cool down. I believe if they had done so, their relationship would have remained intact. Strife and separation would not have taken place between them.

The Bible gives us clear instructions about how to handle strife. The scriptures listed below offer preventative measures we can take to reduce our risk of getting into strife. Remember, the person who decides to do the work will be the one who gets the results.

"A wrathful man stirreth up strife: but he that is slow to anger appeaseth strife." (Proverbs 15:18)

"The beginning of strife is as when one letteth out water: therefore leave off contention, before it be meddled with." (Proverbs 17:14)

"Cast out the scorner, and contention shall go out; yea, strife and reproach shall cease." (Proverbs 22:10)

"Where no wood is, there the fire goeth out: so where there is no talebearer, the strife ceaseth." (Proverbs 26:20)

"He that is of a proud heart stirreth up strife." (Proverbs 28:25a)

Proverbs 20:3a sums it up beautifully when it says it's an honor to cease from strife. If you find yourself in strife, stop! It's not worth the heartache and the pain it causes. I've seen people physically get hurt because one word led to the next word, and before you knew it, somebody was hit in the mouth. Have you ever wondered why a person would hit another in the mouth? It's because they are trying to stop them from talking. They can't take another word from them. It's the best way to shut them up. More people have been physically injured over words than all fatal diseases combined. People have been killed because of strife. It doesn't have to happen to you or me. Somebody has to be quiet before it goes too far. You and I have the power to turn it around whenever we choose. The best thing to do is to avoid conflict. Don't get involved with any form of strife. We must not allow the voice of the flesh to continue setting us back in this area. Meditate on the scriptures above. They will help you avoid getting lured into strife.

Here are a few more scriptures to meditate on in reference to your mouth and the words that come from it.

"Put away from thee a forward mouth, and perverse lips put far from thee." (Proverbs 4:24)

"Thou art snared with the words of thy mouth, thou art taken with the words of thy mouth." (Proverbs 6:2)

"He that keepeth his mouth keepeth his life: but he that openeth wide his lips shall have destruction." (Proverbs 13:3)

"Let no corrupt communication proceed out of your mouth, but that which is good to the use of edifying, that it may minister grace unto the hearers." (Ephesians 4:29)

These scriptures will help you control your emotions and keep you from speaking words that cause strife.

CHAPTER 11

VOICE OF THE EMOTIONS

Two scriptures come to mind when I think about the voice of the emotions.

"In your patience possess ye your soul." (Luke 21:19)

"A fool uttereth all his mind: but a wise man keepeth it in till afterwards." (Proverbs 29:11)

The fool runs his mouth, saying things that he shouldn't because he's emotional. There are several negative characteristics that you need to recognize to know when the voice of the emotions is speaking to you. Let's look at four of them.

Your emotions are extremely self-centered and very strong-willed.

Their focus is self-gratification. Once a person becomes emotionally involved with something, it is extremely difficult for them to let it go. It's all about them and what they want, when they want it, and how they want it. Because the emotions are self-centered, they can blind you and cause self-deception.

Your emotions can be very deceptive.

Your emotions can blind you from seeing the truth. This voice will convince you that you are right and everybody else is wrong. It can cause you to harm others as well as yourself. People don't harm themselves or others until they get extremely emotional about something. Your emotions can take you to great heights or the deepest depths of sorrow. Before people get suicidal, they become emotional first. Then the devil uses these emotions against them to destroy their lives.

Your emotions can make you unaccountable.

When your emotions are out of control, you are not willing to make yourself accountable to anything or anybody. The thought process is, "I'm going to do what I feel like doing, and nobody is going to stop me." There are generally no boundaries. It's whatever I'm big and bad enough to do.

Your emotions can cause you to hold on to pain.

When a person is emotional, they don't let things go easily. This voice will cause individuals to hold on to things until it makes them sick, and they still won't let them go. Sometimes people hold on to things that take them straight to the grave. They literally hold on to them until it kills them. And some people are even holding things against the dead. The person who hurt them has passed away, yet they are still holding on to the pain.

God taught me a very useful principle concerning letting things go. He told me, "Whatever you let go of will let go of you, and whatever you hold on to will hold on to you." This principle reminds me of what the Bible says in Matthew 18:18: "Verily I say unto you, whatsoever ye shall bind on earth shall be bound in heaven and whatsoever ye shall loose on earth shall be loosed in heaven."

Whatever you let go of will lose you. Whatever you hold on to will bind itself to you. Simply put, if you let it go, it will let you go. You will become free from it. If you hold on to it, it will attach itself to you. It will restrain or restrict you. You will become a prisoner, controlled by its every command. When using this principle of letting go, you have to talk to yourself. You must tell yourself, *I let it go.* The negative thoughts and emotions will still be there, but you must continually say, *I let it go.* The voice of the emotions will tell you things such as, *You don't need to let that go. Don't let them get away with that. Make them pay for what they did to you.*

Every time you have a negative thought or feeling about what happens, you must say to yourself, *I let it go.* Within thirty minutes, you will feel yourself being freed from the negative control of your emotions. The thoughts will dissipate over time until they are completely gone. This principle has worked for me 100 percent of the time. And it will work for you as well if you are consistent. Don't back down from the negative thoughts and feelings. Fight back by saying, *I let it go,* and your victory will manifest sooner than you think.

I remember working at a well-known bank in Charlotte, NC. It was difficult to get a job at this financial institution. When people get employed there, they only leave at retirement. This company is a great employer. I came to the bank as a contractor. My job was to monitor personal transactions and business accounts to detect money laundering or terrorist activity. This was the best job I ever had in corporate America. I loved my job and became very good at it. My peer, Yolonda Reeve, and I became so good at it that our work got the attention of the Senior Executive Director of the department. He would come to visit us often just to talk and share his vision for the Financial Intelligence Unit. One day, he came to visit and said he was creating a position for us to be employed full-time with the company. He also mentioned the base salary, and it was a huge amount of money compared to our current income. His only requirement was for us to be patient with him while he strategically put everything in place. He valued us and did not want anyone to leave to go to work with another company.

This conversation totally locked me in. I could see a future with the company. I wasn't going anywhere. As time passed, everything was still on pace for the transition to full-time employment. The Senior Director constantly visited us and gave us updates. One day he came to visit and said everything was off. The CEO had put a hiring freeze on new employment. Compensation and retirement packages were being issued. He said we could have as much time as we needed to look for employment. We had ninety days before our contract ended.

This was truly the most disappointing news I had heard in many years. Emotionally, I was devastated and very hurt. My emotions were all over the place. I immediately started fighting these feelings by telling myself to get a grip on my emotions. I knew in my heart that God had my back and that another job opportunity would become available. Getting another job was not my issue or concern. I was struggling emotionally, and I could not shake the feelings I was experiencing. It was so bad that when I went on my first interview and got the job, I didn't want to be there. I did so well in the interview that I was hired on the spot. The office environment was great. I was working on the trading floor. The department I was working with had a good manager, and the team members were very nice. The money was good as well. This bank was well-known globally. I had all of this, and yet I didn't want to be there. I was experiencing separation and loss at a level that I had never known before. I wasn't this emotional when my father passed. I'm just trying to give you a picture of how emotional I became over a job. This way, you can appreciate how God brought me out. He taught me a principle that will work no matter where you are emotionally.

While working with the new financial institution for a month, I was tormented day and night by the voice of my emotions. I was not getting any major relief at all. I didn't have any peace in this area of my life. I experienced peace in other areas, such as family, church, relationships, and business. But my job was wearing me out. It just goes to show you that a person can function well in some areas of life because of peace but not in other areas where there is no peace. What you need to be mindful of is that if you don't get over it soon, the lack of peace in one area will start affecting the others. It will be a subtle shift, and before you know it, you will start experiencing a lack of peace in all areas where peace once ruled.

The Holy Spirit was not causing a lack of peace. He was trying to get me back to a place of comfort and peace. I was the problem. I was holding on to something that was over and was unwilling to accept it. It reminds me of past relationships that my friends told me about that didn't work out as expected. They were not willing to move on. They wanted something that was over to continue. Many of us have experienced this. Disappointment and pain don't go away overnight. If we jump into another relationship too soon, we carry the past with us, which is unfair to the other person. This is how I felt. I carried some emotional pain into my next job and didn't want to give the new bank an opportunity to show me how good I had it.

I thank God that He didn't give up on me. He gave me mercy and grace. He rebuked me in love and then gave me a principle that changed my life. I still use it today, and it has worked extremely well over many years. When I first used the Let Go Principle, I was free within hours. I excelled on the job and was hired full-time several months later with a very nice income. God is good to those who put their trust in him.

A practical example of how to practice the principle would be that if you were upset with someone because they said something that hurt your feelings, you must immediately say, "I let it go." If the thought of what they said comes to your mind again, then say again, "I let it go." Every time you have a negative feeling or thought, verbally say, "I let it go." Shortly, you will notice how the words that were spoken to you, and the hurt they caused, begin to decrease in their power to control you. The emotional grip begins to weaken, and before long, you will be free of it. Practicing this principle has changed my life dramatically. I encourage you to make this a part of your life so that you can remain free and experience success mentally and emotionally.

The voice of the emotions is extremely dangerous and the hardest to control. It's all about how it makes you feel in your soul and body. It's the total feeling of the physical body and the emotional experience. This is a dangerous combination to have to deal with daily because emotions can affect the body. As a result, the body can affect your emotions. They are partners in crime. When you see or hear one, the other is present as well.

An important fact to remember is that God will never lead you by your emotions. For example, have you ever felt good about something and believed it came from God? Later, you found out that God was not in it at all. You wondered, how did you miss it? You really felt good about it, but it was a big blunder and definitely embarrassing.

We should be careful about saying things like, I feel good about this, or I feel good about it in my spirit. First of all, your spirit is incapable of feeling anything. Proverbs 18:14 says, "The spirit of a man will sustain his infirmity; but a wounded spirit, who can bear?" If a man's spirit is capable of emotions, there is no way it could sustain him because his emotions would overtake him. This reaction would cause him to succumb to whatever he is facing. Your spirit is not emotional. Your soul is where your feelings are located. It is the place where you can experience every kind of emotion known to man. You must understand that man is a three-part being: spirit, soul, and body. The spirit of the man is vastly different from the soul. Please don't get them confused.

Have you ever had moments in your Christian walk with God when you experienced a feeling of excitement about something? You were sure that God was leading you because of how good you felt about it. Being excited and enthusiastic about a thing is never a good indication that God is leading you to do something. All of us have been duped by our feelings, by thinking, since I feel good about it, it must be God! We have deceived ourselves by thinking that God leads us by our emotions. This is a hard lesson to learn, and it can be costly.

We need to be careful of constantly saying, "I really feel good about this." Your feelings are not a solid indication that you are making the right spiritual or natural decision.

Your feelings will deceive you every time when it comes to spiritual matters. You can consider saying, "I perceive in my spirit this is the right thing to do," instead of "I feel good about making this decision." We even ask our spouse or friends, when faced with a decision, "How do you feel about it?" Your feelings should never have anything to do with how you make decisions.

You could say, "I have a witness in my spirit," or "I perceive in my spirit that I should do this or that." Observe the wording in the following scripture.

> "The Spirit itself beareth witness with our spirit that we are the children of God." (Romans 8:19)

> "This is he that came by water and blood, even Jesus Christ; not by water only but by water and blood. And it is the Spirit that beareth witness, because the Spirit is truth." (I John 5:6)

> "And the Lord called Samuel again the third time. And he arose and went to Eli, and said, here am I; for thou didst call me. And Eli perceived that the Lord had called the child." (I Samuel 3:8)

"And immediately when Jesus perceived in his spirit that they so reasoned within themselves, he said unto them, Why reason ye these things in your hearts?" (Mark 2:8)

Jesus perceived what was in their hearts. Eli perceived that the Lord had called Samuel. We should be very careful of the words we choose to say in relation to discerning God's voice when He leads us in a certain direction. Words are very powerful, and we should be mindful of how we use them. To say, "I feel good about this," provokes your emotions. Remember, your emotions are not reliable when it comes to making decisions.

CHAPTER 12

VOICE OF REASONING

The Bible says in Romans 8:6-7, "For to be carnally minded is death; but to be spiritually minded is life and peace. Because the carnal mind is enmity against God: for it is not subject to the law of God, neither indeed can be."

The voice of reasoning is the most dangerous of all for Christians as it pertains to their relationship with God. Mark 8:14-21 says:

> "Now the disciples had forgotten to take bread, neither had they in the ship with them more than one loaf. And he charged them, saying, take heed, beware of the leaven of the Pharisees, and the leaven of Herod. And they reasoned among themselves, saying, it is because we have no bread. And when Jesus knew it, he saith unto them, why reason ye, because ye have no bread? Perceive ye not yet, neither understand? Have ye your heart yet hardened? Having eyes, see ye not? And having ears, hear ye not? And do ye not remember? When I brake the five loaves among five thousand, how many baskets full of fragments took ye up? They say unto him, Twelve. And when the seven among four thousand, how

many baskets full of fragment took ye up? They said, seven. And he said unto them, how is it that ye do not understand?"

This voice of reason keeps you from hearing, seeing, and understanding spiritual truths. It talks you out of accepting the will of God for your life. It keeps you sick, broke, frustrated, and depressed. The voice of reason can also keep you confused about what God said concerning a specific matter. It will have you wondering, is this God, or is this me talking?

This voice is ruled by the five physical senses. Everything has to make sense! If it doesn't, the brain becomes confused and fights to make sense of everything. Your conscious mind goes into shut-down mode and locks you into what you have been taught and trained to believe. Reasoning is the place or process of analysis and decision-making skills. There is no place for reasoning in the spiritual realm. In the physical or natural world, it works very well. It was designed or created to have a position of authority in your life. It has kept us safe, and we have been trained to rely on it. The problem is that we've allowed it to rule our entire being: spirit, soul, and body.

The voice of reason is a large part of who you are. You have allowed that part of you to speak and control you all of your life. It's your ego, your self-image, and the total sum of all the things you have learned and been trained to do on a conscious level. This voice is all about maintaining control over you. Listen to how it talks: *I thrive on maintaining control. Things that don't make sense mean that I lose control. If I lose control, I become afraid and very uncomfortable. To lose control means to depend on something I can't see, hear, or touch. I have not been trained for this. Therefore, I will not allow it.*

The voice of reason is part of the struggle behind why it's so hard to walk by faith and not by sight. Living a life of faith is a slow process for most Christians. And that's because we are sense-ruled by the voice of reason. The voice of reason fights against anything that involves faith. The Bible teaches us to walk by faith and not by sight. We must remember that our entire life has been governed by the five physical senses. We have been trained to operate in this natural world where our senses are in control of what we do. The truth is that to operate or live outside of the sense realm is painful and initially difficult to do. But we can do all things through Christ which strengthens us. We must re-enroll in God's spiritual boot camp so that we can be trained to live in the spirit.

The more you obey God from your spirit, the easier it becomes to keep the voice of reason quiet. The reality is that it will never go away. It will always be a part of you. It will only usurp authority in areas of your life that you are not willing to change. Training yourself to be led by the Spirit causes the voice of reason to speak less. When it does speak, it's not loud. Neither does it speak with authority. Maintaining control in this area allows your spirit to be the prevailing force in your life. Even though the voice of reason will always be a part of you, it must be submissive to your spirit. The voice of reason's primary function is to help navigate you through this phys-ical world. It has no business being involved in spiritual matters. We must keep it in its place.

Let's look at the story of David and Bathsheba in II Samuel 11:1-17 as an example of the voices of the flesh, emotions, and reason working together to bring about a catastrophic event.

The voice of the flesh

II Samuel 11:2 provides a good example of how the voice of the flesh was strengthened through the eyes. David saw Bathsheba bathing herself, and she was very beautiful to look upon. Because King David looked too long, it stirred up his flesh. The Bible tells us in I John 2:16, "For all that is in the world, the lust of the flesh, and the lust of the eyes, and the pride of life, is not of the Father, but is of the world." As Christians, we cannot get caught up in the things of this world. The world will present to us things that are pleasing to the flesh and pleasant to the eyes to trap us. The end result of this is death.

The voice of the emotions

She was very beautiful to David. He watched so long that he began to crave her and felt a strong emotional desire to have her. This is a good example of how what we see can cause an emotional attachment. This is why we must discipline ourselves when it comes to what we look at and how long we look at it. The media, particularly TV, has a lot of things to present to the Christian community that is pleasant to the eyes. What we see feeds the emotions and causes us to yield to ungodly things. We must monitor what we look at on TV. If we don't, it could be a life-altering experience for the worst. The lust for other things can enter in and choke the word, and it will become unfruitful in your life. (Mark 4:19)

The voice of reason

In II Samuel 11:3-4, King David has already decided in his mind that he wants her. He had already yielded to his flesh and emotions. He allowed these voices to convince him that he must have her. At this point, the voice of reasoning begins to speak. I can imagine it saying, *I am the King, and I can have whatever I want, and no one will deny me*. So, King David started gathering information about Bathsheba so that he could figure out how he could pull this off. He found out her name and had a messenger go to get her. He then laid with her, and Bathsheba became pregnant. When David's plan for her husband Uriah to lay with his wife did not work out, David had him killed in battle. Do you see how the voice of reason was the commanding voice and how it spun a web around David? It caused him to make an unreasonable decision to cover up his sins by murdering a man.

All of us have experienced being caught in a web spun by the voice of reason. You may be in a situation now where you feel trapped on every side. It may appear that everything is closing in on you. Every time you try to fix it, it only gets worse. Don't keep digging yourself into a deeper hole as King David did. Stop and ask God to help you be honest and truthful to those whom you have deceived. He will help you if you mean it from your heart. He will deliver you even though you may experience some embarrassing moments. God will always exalt an individual who humbles himself. So, humble yourself so that you may be exalted in due time (I Peter 5:6).

CHAPTER 13

VOICE OF THE DEVIL

I will not say much about the devil speaking to you because it's easy to recognize his voice. Even unbelievers know his voice. They will say something like, "The devil told me to do that." Any voice that condemns you, makes you feel guilty and unworthy, tells you to harm yourself and others, and attempts to separate you from God is the voice of the devil. It's not hard to recognize his voice.

Now, where it can get difficult to detect him is when he hides behind other voices and causes you to think it's you talking. The fact that we have been trained all of our lives to obey these voices makes it easy for him to send you a message without the source being recognized. He can seduce you through these voices and cause you to be in an emotional rage. Once he gets you to this point, there is the possibility that you want to kill someone. All along, he's making you think that you were only angry. Being angry to the point of wanting to kill someone—that's the devil, not you. This means you have to be sharp at knowing who's talking and causing you to have these negative behaviors. Before you act, examine what's being said, the nature of the argument that's presented, and who's behind it. If you take the time to silence yourself and focus, you will be able to discern where the voice is coming from. Then it's up to you to be obedient to God or to the works of the devil.

The devil's primary goal is to tell you things that separate you from God's love. He attacks the relationship that you have with God. He wants you to leave God because he knows that God will never leave you. He uses the guilt of sin and your unworthiness of God's forgiveness and love to create the separation. Then he will attempt to destroy you.

The Bible says in John 10:10, "The thief cometh not but for to steal, and to kill, and to destroy: I am come that they might have life, and that they might have it more abundantly." The devil can, at any time, intertwine his voice with the voice of the flesh, the voice of the emotion, and the voice of reason. This is what makes it difficult to detect his movements of deceitfulness. Remember, we have been programmed our entire lives to depend on all of these voices to operate in the natural world. This is why it's so hard to break ties with them.

Hopefully, at this point, you can recognize what is truly going on behind the scenes. The enemy of your soul is strategically maneuvering in and out of these voices to disguise himself. He wants you to think that the thoughts he is projecting in your mind are your thoughts. He does not want you to know they're coming from him. He's a thief, and a good thief never reveals himself. He always wants to remain unknown so that he can steal again and not be detected.

Let's talk about how the devil deceived Eve in the Garden of Eden and how he used the voice of the flesh, the voice of reason, and the voice of the emotions to separate Eve from God. In Genesis 3:1-13, the story begins with the devil questioning what God said to Eve about the fruit on the tree in the midst of the Garden. He prodded her to listen to his reasoning. The devil told her, "Ye shall not surely die. For God doth know that in the day ye eat thereof, then your eyes shall be opened, and ye shall be as gods, knowing good and evil." The devil planted the seed of reasoning. Eve began to think about it within herself. The voice of reasoning took over, and her flesh and emotions followed. She saw the tree was good for food and that it was pleasant to the eyes. And it was good to make one wise. She was so physically and emotionally attracted to the fruit of the tree that she disobeyed God and ate it. Then she gave it to Adam, and he ate of the fruit as well. Notice how the devil deceived her through two of the five physical senses. He caused her to see the fruit in a way that she never saw it before. The words that he used to lure her were full of deceit: "You will not die. When you eat it, you will be as a god." The words she heard lured her into pride.

I am going to share a testimony of how the devil used the same strategy on me that he used to deceive Eve. He doesn't have any new tricks. He doesn't need any new ways of deceiving people. Why? It is because he's deceiving enough people by using the same tricks over and over again. Why would he need to come up with something new when what he's doing is working? I am not glorifying the devil. The evidence can be seen right outside your front door. In some cases, it is in your house staring at you through the mirror when you wake up in the morning. Sometimes, we allow the devil to use us as weapons of evil works, such as strife, division, jealousy, anger, pride, deceit, and a host of other ungodly things.

This story that I share with you shows how the enemy used the same deceptive trick on me that he did on Eve in the Garden of Eden.

Abby and I attended Carmel Junior High school together in Charlotte, NC. Abby was very attractive, but she was out of my league. Even though she knew me, she was not attracted to me at all. She liked the bad boy type of guys, and I wasn't that kind of person. The following year, I went to another school, and I never saw her again. During the next three years, I would run into guys from high school, and I would ask about Abby. They would tell me that she was still looking good, even after having a baby.

After graduating from high school, I joined the Army. While I was there, I gave my life to the Lord. During the last six months of my time in the Army, I would come home and go to a small Word of Faith church. I really loved the church because I would see the gifts of the Spirit, true worship and the word of God taught and preached with power. Several times while visiting the church, I overheard the preacher talking about this petite woman who came there, and they cast out seven demon spirits from her. They were amazed at how strong she was and that it took three large men to hold her. I found out several weeks later the young lady was Abby. She came back to the church one Sunday while I was there. It was really nice to see her. She shared her testimony with me of how God delivered her and saved her soul. We stayed in touch and talked a lot on the phone. We began to go out to dinner together and spend hours just talking.

I wanted to give you the prelude to how Abby and I met so that everything would make sense as I continue with the story. As the story unfolds, you will see how the devil used the same tactic against me as he did with Eve. He used the five physical senses as a conduit to project his messages through the voice of flesh, voice of emotion, and voice of reasoning. As we pick up the story, Abby and I are sitting in the car talking. We started talking about how we felt about one another. We talked about dating. As we were talking, a thick invisible wall came between us. I felt it block me from her. The more we talked, the thicker it got. You must understand I was a baby Christian, and I didn't know the voice of God or his ways.

As I continued to talk to Abby concerning dating, I heard a voice on the inside of me say, *Don't date her!* It was loud, and I knew in my spirit that it was God. Then, right in the midst of that, God gave me a vision of a 10-foot-thick concrete wall. I saw myself jumping up to the top of the wall to climb over it. As Abby and I continued to talk, I saw myself almost getting to the top of the wall. I was trying vigorously to accomplish this. And God continued to say, *No, don't date her.* God was doing all he could to get my attention and stop me from making a bad mistake. Finally, after about an hour, I reached over and gave her an innocent kiss. When I did this, the wall between us came down instantly, and at the same time, in a vision, I saw myself standing on top of the 10-foot-thick wall. I jumped down on the other side. That was the beginning of hell on earth for me. Things started going downhill in our relationship. The fruit of the Spirit was not flowing to full capacity in our relationship.

By the way, let me mention something to the single person who is reading this book. If you are dating, and the potential for marriage is something you are thinking about, make sure the fruit of the Spirit is prevalent in your relationship. The fruit of the Spirit is a good measuring stick for whether you should get married. Galatians 5:22–23 says, "But the fruit of the Spirit is love, joy, peace, longsuffering, gentleness, goodness, faith, meekness, temperance: against such there is no law." If you don't have the fruit functioning at full capacity in your relationship, you need to wait or maybe you need to move on. When there is no fruit being manifested, run! It will save you from the counterfeit. In 99 percent of relationships, the counterfeit comes before the real thing. You are blessed and highly favored if you are sensitive to the voice of God and pick the right one the first time. Generally, most of us miss it and waste a lot of time choosing our mates instead of asking God to get involved in helping us to choose the person He wants for us.

Let's get back to my testimony about Abby. Yes, things were going downhill. We were arguing a lot, impatient with each other, and found no joy. Peace would come and go. It would stay away from us as though we had a disease. We loved each other, but it became extremely difficult for me because of her carnality. I found out that she didn't love God the same way I did. She did not want the lifestyle it took to serve God the way I did. Both of us were still going to church each week. We were actively involved in church. Before things got really bad, we went to pick out an engagement ring. I put the ring on layaway and made monthly payments. As time went by, I started noticing subtle changes in her behavior. I heard that she was spotted in a crack house. My brother started telling me on several occasions that God is not going to let you marry Abby.

So, I asked God to open my eyes so that I might see what I needed to see. God gave me a dream. I was standing at the altar, and the preacher had announced us as husband and wife. The preacher said, you may now kiss your bride. When I lifted up her veil, a demon spoke out of her and said in a deep man's voice, "I got you now." I told Abby about the dream, and she did not comment on it at all. She was completely silent. I was surprised that she didn't say anything. It was as though what I said about my dream was true. A little time transpired as I was waiting on God to bring the proof that I needed to confront her about her behavior. A dream about a demon speaking through my future wife is not enough to break off the relationship. How crazy would I sound if I told someone I broke off my engagement because I had a dream of a demon speaking through the woman I plan to marry?

My prayer was finally answered. God did exactly what I asked of him. As I was spending a lot of time with God, it became very uncomfortable for Abby to be around me. God finally pulled back the curtain and allowed me to see.

One day, Abby needed transportation to work. I worked in the downtown area of the city of Charlotte. Catching the bus was not a problem. The bus stop was right at my back door. So, I let her use my car to go to work with the stipulation that she had to pick me up at 5:00 p.m. Well, five o'clock came and no Abby. Six o'clock came, and Abby never showed up. So, I caught the bus home. I called her house, and her grandfather did not know where she was. The next day, I didn't hear from her. Abby had stolen my car and kept it for four days. During this time, I knew in my spirit that she was on a drug binge. I called the store where I had her ring on layaway. They told me that she took the ring off layaway and got the money. I don't know how she did this when the account was in my name. Well, she finally called me. She was very apologetic, and I allowed her to talk without losing my cool. I had to stay in control of my emotions so that I could find out the location of my car. She did eventually tell me where it was. When I found it on the side of the road, it was in awful shape on the inside.

I went to her house to confront her in love. Of course, I broke up with her, and I did it without yelling and using demeaning negative words. She expected me to explode, but I didn't. It was over between us, and getting angry about it would be a waste of time and energy. When I told her it was over between us, it felt like shackles fell off me. I felt free, spiritually and physically. My body even felt lighter. I went on with my life, and everything started getting better for me. One day the phone rang, and it was Abby. She told me the reason why we didn't get married was because I spent too much time with God. Now, think about that for a moment!

Let's analyze how Satan used the same strategy on me as he did Eve in the garden. He used my physical senses against me. They were open doors that he came through.

Voice of the flesh

Abby was very attractive to the eyes, and I had always liked her since high school.

Voice of the emotions

I spent many hours talking to her and learning about who she was and what her future plans were. I thoroughly enjoyed the conversations. Abby was not just physically attractive, but she was a strong communicator and very intelligent. This made her interesting to me. She was a young lady who knew what she wanted out of life, and she was achieving her goals. These qualities lured me into having an emotional attachment to her. The devil was telling me that I could build a future with her, that we could have a happy and successful life together. Tony, you should marry her, he said. The devil gave me a long list of reasons why I should do this and how everything would work out beautifully. At this point, I was walking in pride. I could envision what I wanted and what I could do. I did not consult God at all. It was all me, and God was not invited to help me with this decision. That was a terrible mistake. By this time, the devil had me. I took his advice and went forward to bring it to pass.

Voice of reasoning

This voice gave me a list of things that made sense. Abby is a Christian now. God saved her and delivered her from demon possession. She is equally yoked in spiritual things as I am. She goes to the same church as I do. She loves God's word, and she's actively involved in the church. Also, she loves me and wants to be my wife. Why shouldn't I marry her? Everything lines up perfectly. Let's do this!

If it were not for the grace and mercy of God and my willingness to seek his face at the last hour, I would have married Abby. I thank God for giving me a second chance to do it right.

CHAPTER 14

VOICE OF GOD

There are many ways that God speaks to his people: the word of God, the Holy Spirit, fivefold ministry gifts, dreams, visions, and the audible voice of God. I want to focus on the way I believe God is speaking to his people in this generation by the leading voice of the Holy Spirit.

God will always speak primarily through his word, but let's talk about the two primary ways He speaks to us by the Holy Spirit. They are by the *inner witness of the Holy Spirit* and the *inner voice of the Holy Spirit*. In this chapter, we will look at how God speaks to us by the inner witness of the Holy Spirit.

Romans 8:16a says, "The Spirit itself beareth witness with our spirit, that we are the children of God." When you are faced with the challenges of life, and don't know what to do, God's instruction or direction will always bear witness within your spirit rather than your mind or emotions. This means that there will be an agreement, a union, and peace in your spirit about what you need to do. The second part of the verse above says that we are the children of God. You will have peace in your spirit that you are a child of God, and there will be no doubt about it.

One of the functions of the *inner witness* is to get you to avoid something. It leads you away from something and directs you back to a place of peace and comfort. The Holy Spirit can certainly lead you to something that is beneficial for your life. I want to focus on how He causes you to avoid the traps and pitfalls the devil has set for you. I believe avoiding traps is just as important as being led to open doors that change your life. You can never get to the open doors if you don't know how to avoid walking into traps along the way.

There are three distinct promptings by the inner witness of the Holy Spirit. Some of you might be wondering what a prompting is? It's God's way of getting your attention to take action when He speaks to you. *It's an inward perception or intuition that is strong on the inside of you to do something.* Most of the time, it is repeated over and over to you.

There are simple indicators to recognize that God is speaking to you by the inner witness of the Holy Spirit. The three promptings are *uneasiness*, *awareness*, and *disturbance*.

Uneasiness

Uneasiness is the still small voice. It's not loud or forceful. You will have a restlessness in your spirit about the issue. You'll become uncomfortable and bothered about it, and it just keeps coming up over and over again. It seems like it just won't let you go. You can't get away from it. Nor will it allow you to rest because it's in your spirit and in your thoughts, bothering you daily. You can't seem to stop it from speaking to you. It continues to speak to you until you obey or resist it. Once you resist it over a certain period of time, the uneasiness leaves, and the consequences of not obeying this prompting begin to happen. You still have time to obey if you want to, but you will experience some damage because you resisted the voice of God beyond his time limit. For example, it's just like disobeying your parents when you have been told over and over again to do something, but you refused to do it. The consequences of being punished will take place. And then you are given the opportunity to obey them by doing what they told you to do the first time.

Uneasiness is like a mosquito bite. When you're bitten by a mosquito, it stings for a moment, which gets your attention immediately. You begin to see the redness, and it starts to itch. In other words, it gets your attention and causes some focused action from you. As time goes by, the itch comes and goes over and over throughout the day until it eventually goes away. In reality, it causes you to pay attention to the repeated uneasiness: the sting and itch. This is an example of how the Holy Spirit prompts us with uneasiness. He causes an uneasiness in your spirit so that you will pay attention and act accordingly to his directions.

Here's an example of uneasiness. In November 2011, I bought an Infinity Q45 SUV for business purposes. I knew I was going to be laid off, but I was getting a good severance package. I had saved some money, and surely within a year, I would find a job. Plus, the business that I invested in would be up and running, and everybody would be getting paid. I had no worries, except there was an uneasiness in my spirit. I knew it was there, but I thought it was because I was being laid off. It wasn't loud or forceful, but it continued for hours. I also heard a voice within me saying, *This is not right. Wait, don't do this! Something is not right.* We were at the dealership while this was going on in my mind. Everybody was smiling and excited. I continued to ignore the still small voice with reasonable explanations. I was thinking to myself that the company is going to make money. There is a huge need for the services the company provided. Plus, if anything goes wrong, I have a good financial package to fall back on. And surely, within a year, I could find a job in the financial crimes field.

My wife and I signed the papers to purchase the truck and looked at each other with uneasiness in our eyes. We told the chief executive officer (CEO) of the company that we had never done anything like this before. I thought to myself, You must be crazy. We purchased the truck as a business expense to assist with transportation for the executive directors of the company. My wife and I held two of these positions within the company, so it made sense. The truck was handed over to the CEO, and the rest was history.

Less than six months into the business, I realized that I missed God's prompting. The uneasiness was the Holy Spirit telling me not to purchase the truck. The business struggled and did not make any money. Therefore, we could not make the truck payments. That meant that I had to make the payments, or my credit would suffer. I had to take the truck from the company and eventually walk away with $60,000 of debt. It took years to recover from the bad decision of not obeying the still small voice of the Holy Spirit. I believe that it's important that we share testimonies that demonstrate God's blessing for obedience and the cost of disobedience.

So, what is the lesson from this event? If you are uneasy about something, stop and wait. Don't make a decision based on what is reasonable. Your mind and emotions will give you plenty of good reasons why you should do something that you should not do. From a Christian perspective, reasonability should never be a means whereby you make decisions. When you are spiritually prompted by the Holy Spirit and follow his leading, you will always reap success. He will guide you into all truth and show you things to come.

Awareness

Awareness is when the Holy Spirit causes you to recognize something that you didn't see before. This level is where the Holy Spirit takes it up a notch to get your attention so you will respond quickly. This prompting of the Holy Spirit enables a person to take aggressive action against disobedience towards God's specific plan or direction for their life.

When the Holy Spirit manifests himself in this particular prompting, he causes your spiritual sensitivity to be amplified. It's a supernatural awareness that allows you to see clearly your state of disobedience toward God's plan for your life.

It's possible that you can be in disobedience and not be aware of it. Unless the Holy Spirit reveals it to you personally or through the teaching of the word of God by the fivefold ministry gifts, you are oblivious to it. Once the Holy Spirit makes you aware of it, he expects you to act quickly to his instructions. Every time you are disobedient to his specific plan for your life, he causes you to experience a lack of peace.

Any path that you pursue, if there is no peace, is not a path where the Spirit of God is leading the way.

The mission of the Holy Spirit is to cause you to become fully aware of your present state of disobedience toward God's specific plan for your life. The Holy Spirit wants you to act quickly to his instructions so that you can get back to a place of peace and comfort in your relationship with God.

Disturbance

When you find yourself in a place where you have no peace, and your soul is perplexed or immensely vexed, you are at the final level where the Holy Spirit is prompting you to act immediately. He creates a sense of urgency in your spirit to act now! You cannot respond later or when you feel like it. You must respond now! You do not have the luxury of putting it off. God requires your immediate response to his directions. The repercussions of not responding to the prompting of the Holy Spirit at this level are very costly. You may never recover; if you do, it could take many years.

Disturbance is like a wasp. Have you ever had a wasp that flew inside your car when you were driving? Whether it's on the front or the back windshield, you are definitely disturbed.

The first thing you think about is being stung. Or if the wasp starts to fly between the back and front windshield of the vehicle, this could cause you to swing at it, and the probability of an accident occurring increases. Having a wasp in your car can be a frightening experience. It causes panic and also an immediate disturbance in your peace to the point that your peace vanishes. It will not return until the wasp has flown out of the car window or it's killed. Whatever the case, the situation demands immediate attention. Immediate obedience is what the Holy Spirit requires from us on this level of prompting.

An important fact to remember is that the Holy Spirit will occasionally take you from uneasiness through disturbance to give you a chance to act. But there are many times that God speaks to you by the Holy Spirit, and you can be at the disturbance level immediately. It is according to as the Spirit of God wills. It's not a step-by-step process. So, don't get caught up in that. Just understand which stage of the process you are in and then act accordingly.

In my following testimony, I will explain exactly what stage of the prompting of the Holy Spirit I was in. You will be able to see clearly how the Spirit of God prompted me in a business deal that began bitter but turned out sweet.

Since the business in my earlier testimony could not pay for the truck, I had no choice but to take it back and begin making the payments. I remember once I got the truck back into my possession, my wife and I discussed refinancing the truck to lower the payment. The payment was very high, and we needed some breathing room. So, we decided to go to the bank that financed the truck. We thought, surely, we could get this done there. Our credit was excellent, and we never missed a payment. We arrived there, and the bank turned us down. They said the truck was too old. We went to our personal bank, and we got turned down there as well. They told us the truck was too old. Well, that meant we were stuck with making those high payments. We did this for over two years.

Finally, it came to the point that we needed another car. We decided to trade the truck to get a car. As we were out looking and talking to dealers, suddenly, I was at the disturbance level. Peace had been stripped from me. I was miserable. I was so vexed in my spirit and mind that I was rubbing my head and was full of anxiety. All of a sudden, my wife said, "Let's go to our bank and see if we can get it financed." Right when she said that, peace came. There was an inner calmness. All of the vexation and anxiety were gone immediately. I had an inner knowing in my spirit that it was the right thing to do. I agreed to do it the next day. Remember, the bank had already turned us down two years earlier. The truck is two more years older. To go that route again did not make sense. But I had immediate peace when my wife mentioned it. When we got there, the bank refinanced the truck and freed up $250 from the monthly payment. I used this money to pay off another debt.

Obeying the inner witness of the Holy Spirit through disturbance led me away from something that was not in my best interest and directed me back to a place of peace and comfort.

CHAPTER 15

PEACE:
THE LEADING VOICE OF THE HOLY SPIRIT

God also leads and speaks to us by the inner voice of the Holy Spirit. The question is, how does God do this? Remember, I mentioned previously that God speaks to us from the inside out and not the outside in. His voice doesn't come from the clouds. In other words, his voice comes from within us.

The Bible tells us to be led by the Spirit of God (Romans 8:14). There are two distinct manifestations of the leading voice of the Holy Spirit. They are peace and inner knowing. This is how God speaks and leads his people. It's by his peace and the inner knowing within your spirit.

Let's talk about how God speaks to us through his peace. The Holy Spirit will lead you by the peace of God if you allow him. He has a unique way of doing this. There are a few things that you must become familiar with to be led successfully.

> "Let the peace of God rule in your hearts, to the which also ye are called in one body, and be ye thankful." (Colossians 3:15)

"And the peace of God which passeth all understanding shall keep your hearts and mind through Christ Jesus." (Philippians 4:7)

"Be led forth with Peace." (Isaiah 55:12b)

For the peace of God to rule and direct you, you must recognize it, become familiar with it, and know what it feels like in your spirit, not in your flesh. This peace is not a feeling that's connected with your emotions and physical body, which are influenced by external things. Neither does the peace of God have anything to do with material possessions such as cars, money, houses, and relationships.

The Bible tells us in John 14:27, "Peace I leave with you, my peace I give unto you; not as the world giveth, give I unto you. Let not your heart be troubled, neither let it be afraid." The peace that God gives you is not connected with or influenced by the world. This is a peace that comes from your spirit. It's the kind of peace that's not external or influenced by outside things. It's internal and influenced by spiritual things from the Spirit of God. This is why God, by the Holy Spirit, can lead you through peace.

"For the kingdom of God is not meat and drink;
but righteousness, and peace, and joy in the Holy
Ghost." (Romans 14:17)

So, the question is, how do I recognize God's peace? In other words, how do I know that I am following his peace versus the kind of peace that the world gives? Below are a few indicators of the peace of God, including *calmness*, *quietness or stillness*, and *inner strength*.

Calmness

God's peace is a *calmness* that comes to you like a breath of fresh air, washing from your mind negative thoughts. Sometimes, calmness comes over you like a blanket, causing your mind and body to be relieved of the thoughts that cause doubt, confusion, and stress. You only experience this calmness if you go in the direction the Spirit of God is leading you. Once you pursue that path, peace will overtake you and lead you. Sometimes, God's peace is present upon you before you move in obedience. A thought, suggestion, or idea from the Holy Spirit will come to you, and peace will engulf you; and as you follow where the Holy Spirit leads, peace will remain with you. If you go in another direction, your peace will be disturbed, and you will know it. You will become agitated or troubled. Once you get back on track, your peace will return in full force.

One of the greatest lessons to learn in life, particularly on a spiritual level, is not to make a decision that disturbs your inner peace. If you violate this, you suffer the consequences. Any decision that causes unrest, aggravation, uneasiness, stress, or confusion is not of God. Stop! Reverse your actions and get back on the path of peace.

Remember that you always have a chance to know if you have peace or not before making a decision. If you have an emotional conflict inside of you, stop! Don't make a decision yet. Quiet yourself and search for the peace inside you. Don't rush this process! Peace is always there waiting for us to invite its presence and to be led by it so that success can be inevitable.

Quietness or Stillness

God's peace is a *quietness* or a *stillness*. What I mean by this is that everything stops moving, being busy, and noisy. It's like a hush that comes, and nobody is talking or moving. Let me clarify this a little more. Everything externally is busy, moving, and loud. But internally, everything is quiet. This is a beautiful thing to experience. It enables you to stand on the outside of external things and be detached from them.

This causes you not to have any emotional feelings associated with events. The external things are still happening to you, but you are not being affected by them. This brings an inner strength, which is my next point.

Inner Strength

This inner strength allows you not only to face the various challenges of life but also to defeat them with such resolve and calmness that it amazes people and, most of all, yourself. God's peace brings inner strength to continue to move forward day after day until your enemies are defeated. God's peace in you will defeat your enemies because of the effect it has on your perspective, attitude, and behavior. This inner strength allows faith to be activated at peak capacity. The Bible says in James 2:17, "Even so faith, if it hath not works is dead being alone." This inner strength is the peace that gives you the ability to stay mobile in the middle of life's storms.

I remember working at a certain bank for five years, and a merger took place. The bank that I worked for was bought out by a larger bank. It took a little over a year before my area was affected. In the beginning, we were told not to worry about being laid off. We would not be affected by the merger because they did not have a department like ours. They needed to keep our department because it added value. As time went by, we were told that our area would be downsized. It was quick and swift. I was an operations manager, and I had done some extraordinary things for the company. I thought, surely, I was not going to lose my job. Well, the word got out that fourteen team leaders and seven operations managers would be displaced. I was on the list.

When I heard about it from my manager, peace gripped me quickly. I wasn't angry or emotional. There was a quietness or stillness on the inside of me. Internally, there was silence. It was a shush sound. In my spirit, I sensed not to say a word.

My soul was very calm. There were no loud, negative voices causing panic within me. There was a complete silence and a calmness that I could not explain at that time. Within my spirit, I heard the words, *I got this, don't worry.* Externally, everybody was in a panic. Fear was prevalent everywhere. People were telling me how wrong this was for the company to let me go. Even my manager was saying it was wrong. Three of the team leaders that I trained to become operations managers didn't get displaced, nor did they have a better performance rating than I did. Since I did the department budget, I also knew that I was the highest-paid manager on the team. I figure this was the reason for displacing me versus the new team leaders just promoted to a management position.

It was reasonable for me to get angry because I was being treated unfairly. I had an exit meeting with Human Resources, and they could not give me an answer as to why I was being displaced by a less-experienced manager. Externally, there were a lot of moving pieces around me. The voices were loud, but I was calm. Even when I tried to get angry, I couldn't. Peace had me so quiet on the inside that I could do nothing but yield. I have never experienced this type of peace before. This was a new level of peace that I didn't know existed.

This level of peace gave me such an *internal strength* that I moved on with poise and grace that shocked my peers and all that knew me. This peace sustained me long after I left and through the job-search process. God opened a door for me to learn anti-money laundering and anti-terrorism. This field was very rewarding for me financially. And it's an industry where as long as there are thieves and threats to our nation, I will always have a job. So, as you can see, peace always prevails. When God allows one door to be shut, He will have a better door for you to walk through. Just maintain the peace of God at all costs. Don't give it away because of external circumstances. Peace will always stay where it's welcomed. It will defend and comfort you. It will give you inner strength. Don't ever abandon peace. Hold on to it with everything you've got. If you do so, it will serve you well.

The Bible tells us in Hebrews 11:1, "Now faith is the substance of things hoped for, the evidence of things not seen." Without hope, faith has nothing to reach forward to. It can't find its way to become activated without hope. Faith always sees the end from the beginning because hope draws faith toward the end results. No matter how you start out, faith always sees the end results being positive. No hope, no faith; no faith, no resolution. Peace allows you to remain stabilized in your hope, which enables faith to become activated to produce desired results. God's peace gives you hope. His peace keeps hope alive. Hope tells you that everything is going to be all right.

If you don't remember anything I just shared with you, please remember *to keep your peace and protect it at all costs*. The devil is out to get your peace. If he can get your peace, it will cause you to be troubled, stressed, and fearful. Once he has your peace, your faith is no longer protected, and you will be stripped of it. Peace is faith's protection, and without it, you are vulnerable to believe every lie the devil tells you. What a miserable feeling it is to be without peace. We all have been there, and it's a place where you never want to return.

I recall how much peace I had when I was dating my wife, Wanda. When I think about the lack of peace when I was dating Abby, it astounds me. It's like night and day. I am going to share with you how I met Wanda, how God brought us together, and how his peace was present throughout our relationship.

The story began when I met a guy named William Camp. He was an insurance representative in a company called A.L. Williams. He invited me to a business opportunity meeting the company was having at a hotel in Charlotte, NC. The meeting was exciting and full of energy. Numerous people were being promoted. Checks were shown of the money being made, and large performance plaques were given out. I had never seen anything like it. I said to myself, *I want to be a part of this.*

The top guy in the business called Wanda McKenzie up to the stage. I thought to myself, *Who is this good-looking petite woman.* I noticed that everybody, where I was sitting, was cheering for her, including William Camp, the guy who invited me to the meeting. They called her wonder woman. I tell you what—this little lady was awesome. She was full of energy, a great communicator, and was one of the top producers in the Charlotte area. I noticed as I looked around that other leaders who were previously on the stage were yelling and clapping for her. Then I knew this woman was somebody special.

After the meeting was over, William introduced me to her. She was very pleasant and down to earth. She was a regional vice president of the organization. This was a prestigious position in the company. After talking to Wanda and William, I got involved with the company. But the timing was wrong, and I was not productive at all. I was too busy saving souls and casting out devils. My Christian life was extremely important to me, and I was not letting anything impede my growth. I was having so much fun being a Christian that nothing else mattered. Because of that, I excelled quickly as a believer. My commitment was solid and strong.

I left A.L. Williams for two years. When I came back, the timing was perfect. I saw Wanda again in 1986 at Victory Christian Center while touring their new multipurpose facility. When I saw her, I asked her how the business was going. She said, "Everything is going good, but I need a friend. I need someone who I can trust, who would have my back. My organization has grown, and I have a lot of male representatives that I am over. I have to always be on guard. I just need a friend." I told her that I was planning to come back but didn't know how to get in touch with anybody.

I was pleasantly surprised that she was a member of Victory Christian Center. I shared with Wanda that God led me to Victory Christian Center, and it would be my church home. I told her that I would be her friend, and I would have her back. I knew this would not be a problem for me. I felt the sincerity of her words and the concern of needing a real friend. Also, I could do this easily because I was not interested in her. She was a very attractive woman, but she was not what I was looking for. I was looking for a light-skin woman with long black hair who loved God just as much as I did. Listen, my mother was a light-skin woman with long black hair. This was not some fantasy. I had this image in front of me all my life. Let me keep it real.

Wanda was all business. She was strictly looking for a business partner who she could trust, and that was it. She was not attracted to me at all. She later explained to me, after we started dating, that she was going to marry a businessman who had plenty of money and wore suits every day. Neither one of us looked like the right kind of future spouse. But God had a plan, and He was working it out. We didn't realize at the time what God was up to.

In 1986, I had so many potential ladies to pick from to be my wife, that it was not funny, but scary. So many people were trying to get me married. Friends and family members were arranging dates for me with many Christian young ladies. This got to be very tiring. They meant well, but I knew what type of Christian woman I wanted, and God knew as well. So, I stopped all the dating and put my trust in God to help me pick the right mate for me. I knew I could trust him. I had come out of a bad situation with my former fiancée, Abby, and I could not afford any more setbacks. I just didn't want to deal with any more counterfeits. So, I wrote a note about the wife that I would marry, and I put it in my wallet. The note was based on Genesis 24:14-21. Abraham had commissioned his eldest servant in verses 2 through 4 to find a wife for his son Isaac. The servant prayed and asked God in verse 14:

> "And let it come to pass, that the damsel to whom I shall say, let down thy pitcher, I pray thee, that I may drink; and she shall say, drink, and I will give thy camels drink also: let the same be she that thou hast appointed for thy servant Isaac and thereby shall I know that thou hast showed kindness unto my master. And it came to pass, before he had done speaking, that, behold, Rebekah came out, who was born to Bethuel, son of Milcah, the wife of Nahor, Abraham's brother, with her pitcher upon her shoulder. And the damsel was very fair to look upon, a virgin, neither had any man known her: and she went down to the well, and filled her pitcher, and came up. And the servant ran to meet her, and said, let me, I pray thee, drink a little water of thy pitcher. And she said, Drink, my lord: and she hasted, and let down her pitcher upon her hand, and gave him drink. And when she had done giving him drink, she said, I will draw water for thy camels also, until they have done drinking. And she hasted, and emptied her pitcher into the trough, and ran again unto the well to draw water, and drew for all his camels. And the man wondering at her held his peace, to wit whether the Lord had made his journey prosperous or not."

Let's get back to my note to see how it ties in with the story of Isaac's servant and Rebekah. The note I wrote said, "The wife that God chose for me to marry, when I ask her if she is married, she would say, yes, to Jesus, who is the lover of my soul. Yes, that's you. You have been chosen to be my wife."

A year had passed, and my friendship with Wanda became very tight and solid. We spent a lot of business hours together. Not only was she my boss, but she trained me. I received one promotion after another. She was very good at her job. Even after spending so much time around each other, we still had no romantic interest in one another. We even set ourselves in a prayer of agreement that God would bless each other with a spouse of his choosing. As you can see, we were blind and could not see what God was doing. God hid it from us until he was ready to let us know it.

Then one day in 1987, the blinders were removed, and we saw each other in a different way. I remember asking her if she would like to go with me to a church where I was invited to minister the Word of God. She said, "Yes, I would love to go." After the church service was over, I was driving Wanda home, and I asked her a question. The question was very stupid, in my opinion. I asked her if she was married. I knew she was still single. She was single during the entire year as my trainer. So, as you can see, it wasn't an intelligent question. A puzzling thing happened after asking her that question. She responded with an answer without questioning me at all. She said, "Yes, to Jesus."

She could have said, "Tony, you know I'm not married. Why did you ask me that?" This answer would have been the most logical one. I thought to myself, *She responded perfectly to the first part and didn't question me or look at me strangely at all. I could stop right here and not ask her anything else, and that would be good enough for me.* But I knew that I needed to follow through with the second part of my note. Wait! Just think about this with me for a moment. She could have responded in so many different ways. But she answered it perfectly. When she gave me her answer, I did not say anything further about it, and neither did she.

I drove her home and walked her to the door. It was a nice townhouse where she and her mother lived. She invited me in for some juice, and I remember standing in her kitchen, getting ready to go home. I gave her a hug, and as I began to release my arms from around her, something supernatural happened. A strong presence of God's power started turning like a tornado inside my spirit. It became bigger and turned faster. It came up from my belly and went out of my chest into Wanda. It knocked us back. We were very weak and could barely stand to our feet. We could not explain what happened because it was beyond our understanding.

I immediately dragged my tired, drained body out of her mother's house. Spiritually, I was fine, but mentally and emotionally, I was befuddled. On my way home, I asked God what just happened? I could not find the words to explain it. As I began to ponder it more, it seemed like God had given Wanda a part of me spiritually. It was as though He shared with her a part of my spirit and anointing.

The next day, which was Saturday, I had another speaking engagement, and Wanda went with me. Afterward, on the way home, I asked her, "What did the encounter she had with God last night feel like?" She said, "It felt like God made love to my soul." That was a close enough interpretation for me of what I had written on the note that I was carrying in my wallet.

I immediately pulled the car over, pulled out my wallet, and gave her the note I had written exactly one year earlier to the date. I had written the date at the top of the note. She read it and was shocked. She never questioned it. She received me as her future husband, and I accepted her as my future wife. I never had to ask her to marry me, because the note said it all. There was no way either of us could deny it. I had a peace that transcended all natural understanding. In the natural world, there is no way we could explain what happened because it was a supernatural experience. How could you explain or make sense of a supernatural experience like that?

Both of us had peace and sensed an inner knowing that we were meant to be together as a couple. There weren't any doubts, concerns, or questions about it. We knew it was God. We immediately set up a marriage counseling session with our pastor. The session went very well. We had no challenges, baggage, or issues that needed to be worked out before the marriage. It went very smoothly. We started making wedding plans. We continued to work together in the insurance business during the year. The fruit of the spirit was working at peak capacity. We were doing church activities together, such as participating in the singles ministry and street witnessing team. Wanda and I enjoyed working together doing spiritual things. I finally met a woman who loved God as much as I did. Unlike the previous relationship I was in with Abby, which was a counterfeit, Wanda was the real thing. On May 14, 1988, Wanda and I were married. I thank God for choosing her for me. As a couple, we are still experiencing the supernatural power of God.

There is one important fact that I want to mention before going any further. My experience with God concerning choosing my wife and the note I held in my pocket can be considered a fleece. What is a fleece? Simply put, it is asking God to give you an *external* sign that indicates whether something is his will for you. I want to make this as clear as possible. You should never put out a fleece. I had no idea what I was doing. I was young in the Lord, and God was gracious and merciful to me. I was being pursued by many females. I am not bragging or thinking more highly of myself than I should. This is a fact, and it became an issue for me. I did not want to marry the wrong woman based on physical attributes. My heart was right, but my actions were wrong for putting out a fleece. I am more spiritually mature now. If I had to do it all over again, I would not go in that direction. Putting out a fleece is not for the believer today. We have the Holy Spirit, who will guide and teach us. He will show us the things we need to know.

> "Howbeit when he, the Spirit of truth, is come, he will guide you into all truth: for he shall not speak of himself; but whatsoever he shall hear, that shall he speak: and he will shew you things to come." (John 16:13)

> "But the Comforter, which is the Holy Ghost, whom the Father will send in my name, he shall teach you all things, and bring all things to your remembrance, whatsoever I have said unto you." (John 14:26)

> "But yet have an unction from the Holy One and ye know all things." (I John 2:20)

These scriptures let us know that we are to be directed or led by the Holy Spirit pertaining to life issues. We should not be led by external things, such as a sign or fleece. The devil will give you a sign that directs you down the wrong path. That path leads to destruction. He will deceive you into thinking a fleece is the right thing to do to know God's will for your life. Once he gets you trapped into believing that lie, he can cause you to be confused and angry. You begin to think that God is causing bad things to happen to you. You start to wonder why the fleece you put out didn't work this time. I am admonishing you to stay away from putting out a fleece. It is destructive and not of God.

CHAPTER 16

THE INNER KNOWING

W hat is *inner knowing*? It's a perceived idea or suggestion that comes from the Holy Spirit to your spirit with
clarity and certainty.

I John 2:21 says, "For ye have an unction from the Holy One
and you know all things." What is an unction? An unction is
a perception or intuition of an idea or suggestion that comes
from the Holy Spirit that bears witness with your spirit. In
other words, the idea or suggestion agrees with your *spirit*,
not necessarily with your *head*. Trust me, there is a huge
difference between your head and your spirit, particularly
when it comes to hearing from God. God does not talk to
your head; he speaks to you in your spirit. The nonrenewed
mind cannot wrap itself around the things that God speaks or
reveals to you in your spirit. The mind cannot perceive them.

> "And be not conformed to this world: but be ye
> transformed by the renewing of your mind, that ye
> may prove what is that good, and acceptable, and
> perfect will of God." (Romans 12:2)

As Christians, our minds have to be renewed constantly.
If not, we will not understand spiritual things. It will be
difficult for us to receive from God. The Bible clearly tells us

in I Corinthians 2:14, "But the natural man receiveth not the things of the Spirit of God: for they are foolish unto him: neither can he know them because they are spiritually discerned." This is not just talking about the unbeliever. If we as Christians don't stay in the word daily so that God can work on us mentally, we will struggle to receive insight or revelation from God. When your mind has not been renewed in a certain area, you think like an unbeliever. It will be extremely difficult to get your head around spiritual things. Renewing your mind enables you as a Christian to be free from a life of carnal thinking and carnal behavior. The result of being carnal-minded is death. Being spiritually-minded and allowing God's word to transform your thoughts, leads to life and peace.

Your mind is designed to navigate you in the physical world. If something doesn't make sense, the mind dismisses it. Your spirit is designed to function in the unseen world, the spirit world.

The Bible tells us in Acts 14:9 that Paul perceived the crippled man had faith to be healed. This was not revealed to his head but to his spirit. Jesus perceived them reasoning in their hearts. (Mark 2:8). God revealed this in Jesus' Spirit. The spirit of a man is the candle of the Lord. Therefore, God will always speak to your spirit first and not your head. Your spirit then passes it on to your mind or conscience to ponder. This is where the battle begins, and it ends depending on who you choose to obey. You must quickly choose a side and stand your ground. The Bible clearly gives us direction in Joshua 25:15:

> "And if it seem evil unto you to serve the Lord, choose you this day whom ye will serve; whether the gods which your fathers served that were on the other side of the flood, or the gods of the Amorites, in whose land ye dwell: but as for me and my house, we will serve the Lord."

The problem with us is when we decide to obey God, our mind starts fighting us with statements that make sense. We jump sides and start obeying the devil. Then, when God speaks to our spirit, which brings peace, we jump back on his side. So, this constant jumping back and forth causes us to become double-minded and unstable. The conscious mind, which is the voice of reason, has planted the seed of doubt and fear. We must make a decision—not from our head but from our spirit—that we will obey God and be willing to fight with him.

We must be willing to travel a road we have never been on before. The reality is that the more you obey God and fight on his side, the easier it gets to defeat the mind (the voice of reason). You will have fewer problems with the mind putting up a fight. There will come a day that you experience your mind not fighting you at all in specific areas where you have struggled in the past.

You might be thinking to yourself, *How would I recognize that I am experiencing an inner knowing in my spirit? How do I know for sure what to do when I am faced with a challenging issue?* The answer is peace. You will have a peace about it. The inner knowing will produce the peace of God, and the peace of God produces an inner knowing in your spirit. You should always follow the direction that brings peace. Also, an inner knowing will accompany the peace.

Sometimes this means that you have to take a break from your busy life and sit down somewhere and be quiet so that you can ascertain the direction of peace. Most of the time, you have to quieten the mind and search for peace. This can be challenging at times. But we can do all things through Christ that strengthens us. *Remember, the inner knowing from your spirit and the peace of God go together.* It's a hand and glove situation. One is made for the other, and you can't function or be successful without both of them.

In the late 1990s, my wife, Wanda, started getting black spots on the top of her feet. Her feet became very sore and started burning. These black spots started leaking pus. She could not wear regular shoes. Only bedroom shoes kept her feet comfortable. I prayed for her, and then we went to the emergency room at a nearby hospital. The doctors did not know what she had nor the cause. So, they prescribed some antibiotics for her to take. Over the next two days, I noticed the black spots started spreading on her legs, back, chest, and neck. I heard a still small voice say, *Go get the lotion and rub her down with it for the next three days.* This voice was very calm, and it was not forceful or loud. There was a peace that accompanied these words that were spoken to me. But more than the peace, there was a strong knowing on the inside of me. It was so strong that my mind never got a chance to talk to me about what was said. It was in complete shutdown mode. I never had a battle at all with trying to make sense out of what I was being told to do.

I immediately acted on what I heard, applying a simple cocoa butter lotion to the spots. I knew in my spirit that God was speaking to me. And the results were amazing. After the first night, I saw the spots start to clear up. The second night both legs and her back were clearing up. By the third night, 97 percent of all the black spots were gone. In a week's time, she had none left. Her feet were healed, and she could wear shoes again. Praise God! There was nothing in the lotion that healed her. It was my obedience to God's instructions that manifested the results. I just simply followed the inner knowing inside my spirit. God's power was released and produced the healing that Wanda needed.

Just because you have an inner knowing from the Spirit of God to go in a specific direction doesn't mean it's void of challenges or obstacles to overcome. Some Christians are deceived by the devil in this area. They think that it's going to be smooth sailing when the Holy Spirit leads them, and there's not going be any problems. They think if there are situations and challenges to deal with, that it can't be the Holy Spirit leading them. You cannot get caught up in external things. This is where the devil is most powerful. He wants you to look at what is going on and the challenges you're having. You must stay with the inward knowing. Focus on what you believe was given to you by the leading of the Holy Spirit. Don't allow external obstacles to rob you of what you know on the inside of your spirit.

In the 13th chapter of Numbers, God instructed Moses to send out men to search the land of Canaan. This was the land that God promised the children of Israel. This land was flowing with milk and honey. God was leading them to this land, which he had given them. But there were some obstacles. The people were strong that dwelt in the land. The cities had great walls. The Amalekites, Hittites, Jebusites, Amorites, and Canaanites were living in the land. The sons of Anak, who were giants, lived there as well. The obstacles were great for the children of Israel, but God caused them to overcome every obstacle. God delivered their enemies into their hands. The children of Israel possessed the land that God promised them. No matter what the obstacles are on the way to your promised land or even when you get there, know that greater is He that is in you than he that is in the world. God has given you the power to overcome all of the challenges that you face.

When Jesus was led by an inner knowing from the Spirit into the wilderness to be tempted for forty days, it wasn't easy for him. He experienced several challenges. But it didn't mean that He missed God because He had repeated obstacles to overcome. He faced hunger and the constant assault of the devil. Other obstacles were weather conditions, extreme weakness from lack of food, being alone, the threat of being eaten by wild beasts, and the mental and emotional stress from being in a constant battle with Satan. Even though Jesus was led into the wilderness by the Holy Spirit, He was able to overcome everything He faced.

I remember when I had an inner knowing to attend the school of ministry. I knew beyond a shadow of a doubt that I was supposed to go to school to further my education in ministry. In 1994, my wife and I enrolled at More Than Conquerors College. The transition was very smooth. I had no obstacles that I had to overcome in the beginning. The school was perfect for me. I was amazed at how much I was learning. The instructors were spirit-led and extremely helpful. All of a sudden, after six months, I noticed things beginning to change.

The obstacles started to appear one after another. My wife and I began to experience car issues that led to financial challenges. We also had some problems in our relationship with relatives. Also, we came home one day and found our dog dead. He accidentally hung himself on the back porch. This put my wife in a bad place emotionally. At the time, we didn't have any children, and our dog was a close family member. That's in addition to how hard the subjects became and having to stay up 24 hours at a time to get an assignment completed.

I remember not sleeping for two days while having to complete an assignment and study for a test. Time management was crucial, and I did not use my time wisely. It wasn't that I was spending time doing fun things outside of school. It was managing the assignment load. I wish I could have been able to get some downtime. Any extra time I had was spent staying caught up on assignments and projects. I got better at it as time went by, but in the beginning, it was brutal. So, my obstacles did not start until I was in the middle of the first year. I had plenty of opportunities to quit. I could have easily said, *This could not be God. I don't think I was led by the Holy Spirit to do this. Surely, going to school to improve my spiritual growth isn't supposed to be this hard. Maybe this inner knowing was just something I wanted to do, and I missed God on this one.*

I praise God that I never had any of these kinds of thoughts. I just pressed my way through it and trusted God to take care of my needs. I did just that, and I am so glad I did not allow the obstacles to make me quit. My wife and I graduated, and the Lord opened up amazing doors for us. We had business opportunities with the State of North Carolina, and I was given a leadership role in our local church. More doors opened for me to minister the word at my church and other surrounding churches. Financial increase came our way. By obeying the inner knowing by the Holy Spirit, we were able to experience these blessings.

Obstacles and challenges should never be an indication that God is or is not leading you in a certain direction. The inner knowing inside your spirit and the peace that follows is the key to being able to discern the difference. Sometimes, direction from God is not given instantly. There are times when you must be patient. Don't be hasty. Wait on God to get clarity in the direction that you are taking. Sometimes, it takes longer before the direction is revealed through the inner knowing within your spirit. It's not that God is hiding it from you. He might be trying to get you to spend time with him without the distractions of the world. Or maybe it's just taking you this long to quiet yourself down spiritually to discern the knowing within your spirit.

This knowing within your spirit allows the Holy Spirit to successfully lead you to the place where God desires you to be. I know that a lot of us don't want to be patient and wait on God. Frankly speaking, we want it now, and we don't have time to wait. God is not moved by our impatience. We need to get with his program, or it's going to take longer than we want it to. Like it or not, if you want success, it has to be God's way.

"Wait on the Lord: be of good courage and he shall strengthen thine heart: wait I say on the Lord. (Psalm 27:14)

"I call heaven and earth to record this day against you, that I have set before you life and death, blessing and cursing. Therefore, choose life that both thou and thy seed may live." (Deuteronomy 30:19)

When looking at the millions of Christians around the world, you will see a small percentage of them who experience the blessing of God in the way that He intends. Just as an extreme amount of the wealth in the world is owned by a very small number of people, there are a small number of Christians enjoying the fullness of the promises of God. That's because they aren't willing to pay the price of putting the necessary time into developing a relationship with him. I encourage you to join the small number of Christians who hear and obey God from their *spirit* and not their *head*.

CONCLUSION

There is coming a time, which is already at hand, that you must know the voice of God just as you know your own name. You must know and understand how to be led by the Spirit of God. If not, you will suffer immensely, and it will be your fault. You won't be able to blame the pastor or your parents. You alone are responsible for the unnecessary suffering that you will go through. Why would you do this to yourself? Take the time and learn from God. You are unique and wonderfully made, and God knows exactly how to teach you in a way that you understand.

Give God a chance to prove himself to you and to convince you that it's not hard to know his voice. Actually, the hardest part is obeying what God says to do. It's not being able to recognize his voice when He's talking to you. Obedience is what God requires of us. We have made obeying him so difficult because we will not bring our emotions under subjection to his will. We really need to be careful about whom and what we allow to sit on the throne of our lives. Will it be God? Or will it be our flesh, emotions, reasoning, or the devil?

There is nothing more important than knowing the voice of God for yourself. One of the greatest things you can teach your children is to know his voice. If they know his voice and follow it, they will become successful in every area of life. I sincerely hope that what has been said in this book has helped you to easily discern the voice of God by the leading of the Holy Spirit.

My prayer is that you take the principles in this book and apply them to your life. Be diligent and put in the work. God rewards those who diligently seek him. It's not going to be a quick, instant fix. Don't expect that because quick fixes are not sustainable, and God doesn't operate in this manner. If you really want to know his voice, you will have to sacrifice your time. I understand that most of us are under tough time constraints. But trust me, every second you give to God will be multiplied back to you. Spending time with God to learn his voice is immeasurable. So, reset your mind and roll up your sleeves, as it's going to be a good fight. This is a fight that you will win if you stay consistent.

During the learning process, God will make it fun for you, even in disappointing times when you miss the lesson. Don't concern yourself with the mistakes. Just learn from them and move forward quickly so that you don't get frustrated and quit. Don't be in a hurry; just take your time and learn from him. I promise you that it's worth the journey, and your life will be changed forever in a greater way. Then you will be in a position to teach others how to properly hear and obey the voice of God. *God Bless You.*

ABOUT THE AUTHOR

Tony Douglas was born and raised in Huntersville, NC. He is a devoted husband to his wife, Wanda, and a father of three young adult children, Jordan, Adria, and Jaquan. Outside of spiritual interests, he loves reading self-development books, coaching boxing, spending time with his dog Sasha, and having quiet time.

As a young man at the age of 19, he joined the US Army. There he grew as an individual and became a fine leader. Three of his greatest accomplishments while in the military were attending Basic Leadership School, competing in the 1984 Olympic Boxing Trials, and giving his life to the Lord.

Tony has been a licensed minister since 1998 and is very active in his church. In 2001, Tony became a therapeutic foster parent. He and his wife have devoted 15 years of their life to this work. He has received numerous certifications in this field.

Tony is known for his peaceful personality and patience with people. He is thankful to God for all of the things that he has accomplished.

The voice of God has always been Tony's guiding light. As a result, Tony has reached different heights, which have helped him soar in many different arenas of his life. If you are interested to find out more about how Tony turned his life around and created a passageway for a new life full of abundance, please contact Tony on the following handles:

Reach out to Tony:

Website: tddouglas.com
Email: Tonydouglas611@gmail.com
Facebook: TonyDouglas@DiscerningtheVoiceofGod
Instagram: #tonydouglasauthor
LinkedIn: linkedin.com/in/tony-douglas-a904011a6/

The Workbook:
Discerning the Voice of God by the Leading of the Holy Spirit

This workbook will provide some personal reflections for the reader to uncover hidden spiritual truths about themselves. It will enable them to discover what God's desire is for their life. The reader will be placed on a pathway that will empower them to make permanent changes. These changes will impact their lives forever. Purchase this online today, and journal your thoughts and find your purpose.

Membership Program:
Private Sessions on How to Hear the Voice of God.

This membership program provides a roadmap on how to connect with yourself by becoming more attuned with your goals and the path that God has paved for you. Joining our membership site will ensure that you are placed in a forum that is right for you. Tony also provides one-on-one coaching sessions to provide healing, mastery and education for those who are in need of finding a solution towards creating happy and successful outcomes in their lives. Tony can't wait to hear from you, for more information on these courses, check out his website: **tddouglas.com**, for all upcoming announcements.

Hearts to be Heard

Giving a Voice to Creativity!

With every donation, a voice will be given to
the creativity that lies within the hearts of
our children living with diverse challenges.

By making this difference, children that may
not have been given the opportunity to have their
Heart Heard will have the freedom to create
beautiful works of art and musical creations.

Donate by visiting

HeartstobeHeard.com

We thank you.